Praise for This Far by Grace

"Many people wonder, 'Who am I? Why am I here? Am I a mistake?' This author not only had the questions, but he also found the answers.

In this poignant, compelling story, you'll see why Donald struggled with his "identity" and then discover why he struggles—no more."

June Hunt,
Founder, Hope for The Heart
Author, How to Forgive When You Don't Feel Like It

"I have known Donald Johnson for over 20 years. During the time, I have found him to be an earnest disciple of Jesus Christ, evidencing humility, grace, and a strong desire to share the Good News of salvation through Jesus with others. 'This Far by Grace' is an exciting, honest, and helpful look at one man's life transformed by the grace of God. It will encourage you to trust in God's grace to bless and empower you to experience the fullness of life which Jesus promised us all: "I have come that they may have life and that they may have it more abundantly" (John 10:10).

Rev. Dr. Jerry Lynn, Co-Pastor
Reach Out Fellowship Church
Albany, NY

"Youth will find this book's honesty both brutal and refreshing in these Spirit-soaked pages. Donald Johnson's story is a reminder that while all of us do not start well, we can all finish well in Christ. It is an honest story of redemption."

Benjamin Juliano,
Sophomore, Florida Southern College

"I know Donald Johnson. And I love Donald Johnson. I want to inhale when I am around him, for he carries the aroma of Christ. That is what I love most about him. The same Jesus who spoke creation into existence gave a young Donald a firm identity. The same Jesus who died for billions died for Donald so that He could redeem and restore him. The same Jesus who orchestrates the affairs of nations also created a plan that moved Donald from seeming hopelessness to a person who lifts many eyes to heaven. Yes, if you read 'This Far by Grace,' you will be fascinated with Donald Johnson. But even more, you will be fascinated with a King who makes all things new."

Richard Ross, Ph.D., J.M. Price Chair of
Religious Education, Southwestern Theological Seminary,
Co-founder of The True Love Waits movement,
Author, Youth Ministry that Lasts a Lifetime

The incredible Story
of one man's journey
out of darkness into
God's marvelous light

THIS FAR BY GRACE!

D. L. ELLIS-JOHNSON

WESTBOW
PRESS·
A DIVISION OF THOMAS NELSON
& ZONDERVAN

WestBow Press books may be ordered through booksellers or by contacting:

WestBow Press
A Division of Thomas Nelson & Zondervan
1663 Liberty Drive
Bloomington, IN 47403
www.westbowpress.com
1 (866) 928-1240

ISBN: 978-1-9736-8944-7 (sc)
ISBN: 978-1-9736-8943-0 (e)

Print information available on the last page.

WestBow Press rev. date: 5/05/2020

To

My beloved Mother,
Johnnie Lee (Darden) Watson,
you chose life that I might have it
more abundantly!

Thank you.

"...But where sin increased, grace abounded all the more"
(Romans 5:20).

CONTENTS

ACKNOWLEDGMENTS

I am grateful for all the people-good, bad, and "ugly"-who were involved in my life. You helped me become who I am in Christ today!

I give special thanks and honor to my former pastor and church, Bishop Roy Bryant Senior and The Bible Church of Christ. Bishop, I've always said, *"You taught me how to live."* Thank-you!

I am very appreciative of my former colleagues, supervisors, and administrators in the Westchester County Department of Probation, Westchester County, New York. You knew me "before and after." You accepted, encouraged, protected, and helped me grow all the time! Thank you, Commissioner Rocco A. Pozzi, and Nancy M. Lick, retired Chief of Planning, Research and Staff Development (my immediate boss) for giving me a chance to prove that Christ's redemption works!

I praise my editorial team for your love, kindness, patience, and enormous efforts.

Larena Hurako Jones-Tatum, thank you for being a forever "true friend." Your insight and grammatical help in the manuscript (and my life) are invaluable! You are my "shero" from the 215 Projects... Hallelujah!

Coy Starks, Dallas Theological Seminary, Media Center Director, thank you for your help with this project and others since I've attended DTS. Your time and technical skills are a blessing! May God richly bless you!

Benjamin Juliano, my junior editor and (the spiritual son of my right hand), what a gift you are from God! You spent an incredible amount of time in thoroughly editing this book between your college tasks and academic workload. Your help and heart made the project a real success! You will change many generations. God's Speed!

Larry Joseph Candarelli, my former supervising probation officer, you are the most exceptional editor I know. You redlined and "diced" many of my court reports, but you always made me look good because of your integrity and professionalism. Thank you for being "a saint" through "the thick and thin." God bless you, Brother Deacon!

Also, I'd like to express appreciation for my most recent pastors, Dr. Tony Evans and Dr. Robert Jeffress. Your outstanding leadership, incredible faith, and spiritual gifts propel me forward in God's Kingdom agenda. I am convinced that God's pathway is victorious. Tremendous honor, and thanks to each of you!

And finally, to my family and friends, thank you for your prayers, faith, and hope. You believed God! I am saved, delivered, and healed as the results. Hallelujah forever more!!!

Foreword

Minister Donald L. Ellis-Johnson writes this book carefully and thoughtfully. He shows us how God's Hand is over our lives in every situation. It's refreshing to know that we are not an accident or an incident. God has a plan for our lives. He knew who we were before He created us. *"Before I formed thee in the belly, I knew thee; and before thou camest out of the womb, I sanctified thee, and ordained thee a prophet unto the nations" (Jeremiah 1:5 KJV).*

Minister Johnson shares with us his personal story of how God took a perceived tragedy and turned it into a triumph! I use the word "perceived" because God can turn "bad" into good. God's ways are not like our ways. *"For my thoughts are not your thoughts, neither are your ways my ways, saith the Lord. For as the heavens are higher than the earth, so are my ways higher than your ways, and my thoughts than your thoughts" (Isaiah 55:8-9 KJV).*

We have an identity crisis in our world today. People are motivated by what they *THINK,* even if their notion is wrong. The world needs to hear how God can genuinely mold someone from an abandoned and confused soul into a mighty person of valor. *"For as he thinketh in his heart so is he" (Proverbs 23:7 KJV).* As you read this book, put your seatbelts on because God will highlight how you, too, can be transformed.

Remember the experiments our science teachers taught us in school? We raised caterpillars that wrapped themselves in cocoons for weeks. Then, after a transformation process, the caterpillars emerged as beautiful butterflies. Caterpillars release enzymes that dissolve most of their bodies while undergoing this transforming process. They consume proteins, minerals & vitamins while they develop and mature the body parts of butterflies. The caterpillars' new bodies have nothing in common with their old ones. They have fresh legs, organs & a new reproductive system. Even their digestive system does not work the same as their appetite has changed from eating leaves to ingesting nectar.

A similar process is true for born-again believers. We are changed. *"I beseech you therefore, brethren, by the mercies of God, that ye present your bodies a living sacrifice, holy, acceptable unto God, which is your reasonable service. And be not conformed to this world: but be ye transformed by the renewing of your mind, that ye may prove what is that good, and acceptable, and perfect, will of God"* (Romans KJV).

My prayer for you as you read this book is that it will transform you. Someone's mind is getting ready to change. Your perception of yourself and the world will be different. Your attitude will emerge new. Your understanding of God's will and purpose for your life will increase. You will even look different after you read this book! So be encouraged. Let him make you brand new.

Bishop Derek G. Owens, D.D., Senior Pastor
Golden Sword International Fellowship Church
Bronxville, New York

PREFACE

Everyone loves a story. A saga is compelling. It can make one laugh, cry, hate, hope, fear, and reflect. A novel gives a perspective to real-life alongside its revealed truth or fiction. Every person has a story. It begins before you and I are born, and a personal narrative often extends past our physical lives. A story has its own experience! Here, I want to share mine.

My story reveals God's infinite grace, divine favor, mercy, and love. It explains how a person can overcome their destructive inclinations, desires, and sins. God has the sovereign power to save a depraved life, and he can redeem the life that Satan comes to steal, kill, and destroy. God's grace is immeasurable!

My autobiography is about rejection, abandonment, fear, identity conflicts, anger, addiction, and so much more! Yet, it is also an account of God's unfailing love and forgiveness. My story is true!

I am an ordinary person, but thanks be to God, I have triumphed over fear, sin, and Satan's rulership. In reading this book, I hope you will understand and believe you, too, can be an overcomer, more than "a conqueror" through Jesus Christ, who loves us. God can do more than we ask or think, and his grace is sufficient. I am a witness! I have come this far by his grace!

"For God so loved the world, that he gave his only Son, that whoever believes in him should not perish but have eternal life"
(John 3:16).

God bless you,
Minister Donald Ellis-Johnson
March 1, 2020.

INTRODUCTION

God is amazing, and so is his grace! Grace is his unmerited favor. God deals with people and circumstances with grace, and it is a demonstration of God the Superior "stooping down" to bless an inferior (you and me). God's actions are not the results of our goodness. Instead, they are the consequences of his generosity and kindness toward us as he dispenses his mercy, love, truth, and grace. He supplies us with undeserved favor, [1] and his grace is beyond our full comprehension. God's grace surpasses both our knowledge and time, and it intercepts every dimension of history. His grace changes the world.

The first mention of *grace* in the Bible is in the Genesis text (6:5-8). This text depicts the world's condition during the patriarch Noah's generation. The world's evil and sin escalate in Noah's time.

Beforehand, sin enters the world as the consequence of Adam and Eve's disobedience to God's commandment early on in human history. God gives the instruction, but the man and woman choose to disobey. "You may surely eat of every tree of the garden, but of the tree of knowledge of good and evil you shall not eat it...So when the woman saw that the tree was good for food, and that it was a delight to the eyes, and that the tree was to be desired to make one wise, she took of its fruit and ate, and she also gave some to her husband who was with her, and he ate. Then the eyes of both were opened, and they knew that they were naked" (Genesis 2:16-17 and 3:6-7). As Adam and Eve overstep God's divine boundary, sin enters the world. The curse of sin brings corruption and wickedness to humanity, and the created order from that point forward. Sin's implications linger.

Noah's generation is the tenth from Adam's. God, in divine righteous anger, grieves in his heart and regrets he created man. "The LORD saw that the wickedness of man was great in the earth and that every intention of the thoughts of his heart was only evil continually. And the Lord was sorry that he had made man on the earth, and it grieved him to his heart" (Genesis 6:5-6). As such, in Noah's time, God makes an executive decision (judgment) to destroy everything he had created on the earth (Genesis 6:7). How sad!

I think we can imagine somewhat how God feels. It must break God's heart to see people created in his image and likeness (his representatives in the earth) disregard his holiness and violate his will. It impedes his purposes, and what a tragedy that is! But wait, God is good! There is a divine intervention! Remember God's grace? The text continues: "But Noah found favor (*grace)* in the eyes of the Lord" (Genesis 6:8).

Noah's practice of godliness, righteousness, and justice brought him into favor (grace) with God. His godly lifestyle changed the outcome of God's universal judgment. Noah's faithfulness to God served to turn a tragedy into triumph! God spares Noah and his family during a universal flood, and he uses the family to repopulate the earth in the judgment's aftermath (Genesis 7-10). God, in his independent, sufficient, self-existence, does not seek his good but that for others.[2] His grace is sufficient!

Remarkably throughout human history, God demonstrates his love, mercy, and grace. Jesus steps physically into the world in the fullness of time and manifests God's presence and salvation. God says to Joseph, "Do not fear to take Mary as your wife, for that which is conceived in her is from the Holy Spirit. She will bear a son, and you shall call him Jesus, for he will save his people from their sins" (Matthew 1:20-21). God's incarnation in Jesus and his embodiment of unconditional love and grace changes everything. It revises history! "For the law was given through Moses; grace and truth came through Jesus Christ" (John 1:17).

Sacrificially, Christ offers his life for humanity's sins. His death and resurrection provide divine satisfaction for sins' penalty before God, and our redemption and salvation. Today, God's love is present to redeem and save people from eternal death and destruction. "Fear not, for behold, I bring you good news of great joy that will be for all people. For unto you is born this day in the city of David, a Savior who is Christ the Lord" (Luke 2:10-11). God's grace is amazing.

Jesus Christ not only saves people, but his salvation and redemption changes and transforms them too. Christ's death and resurrection liberate people from spiritual and eternal death. His ministry provides an abundant life and freedom from guilt, shame, and an eternal death sentence. Jesus is the way, the truth, and the life, and he gives eternal life to all who accept him as their Savior and Lord.

"I am the door. If anyone enters by me, he will be saved and will go in and out and find pasture..I am the good shepherd"
(John 10:9,11).

1

Who am I?

"*Donald Darden, Donald Darden?* the kindergarten teacher called as she took classroom attendance. "*Donald Darden, are you present?*" I didn't know if I should answer. I was shocked. My name was not Donald Darden; why didn't my teacher know that? My name was changed.

For the first five years of my life, everyone had made the same mistake. The pediatrician, people in family court, the health clinic nurse, people at the Board of Education, all of them made the same mistake, and they called me Donald Darden! Other times, people didn't bother with my last name out of uncertainty or embarrassment because they didn't know my last name. But now, everything was fine. It was fixed, or so I thought it was.

My name was changed at least one month before kindergarten started. Now, after five years, my name was what it was supposed to be- Donald Johnson. How could my teacher make such a mistake, and cause my first day in school to be a disaster?

I had been anxious to start school in Nathan Hale Elementary on Mount Victory's South Side, and I loved to learn. I had committed to be a good student, and I wanted to be one of my teacher's "favorites." I couldn't wait for the opportunity to bring her an apple. It was a warm fall day when I arrived at the two-story brick antique-looking building to start school, and I couldn't imagine anything would be wrong.

My kindergarten classroom was neat and well-equipped with several desks and cubby holes. I wanted to get started, and I would respond robustly when my teacher took the attendance roll. *Donald Johnson* was present and ready for school. Unfortunately, my expectations were shattered.

A slender bright-skinned African American boy with glaring light brown eyes, I wanted to stand up and yell at my teacher, *"My name isn't Donald Darden. It's Donald Johnson!"* I had a very bad and confusing day on the first day of school.

The teacher repeated the third time, *"Donald Darden, Donald Darden; are you present?"* I sat silently in my chair as my heart continued to plummet. Disappointed, I raised my hand and said, *"Present."* I felt forced to make allegiance with a false identity as I put my hand down. I was sick and tired of being called Donald Darden.

Finally, my last name was Johnson, the same as Ma's and Dad's last name. Not only did Ma tell me about it, but I also saw the five-by-five legal paper from the Family Court with my real name *Donald Johnson* on it. Why didn't *everybody* know that?

I tried to figure out what went wrong on the first day of school, and I had a lot of questions. *How could my kindergarten teacher make such a mistake? Why do I have two last names? Is someone to blame? Why was I born? Why am I confused?* I questioned. But God never made a mistake! I needed to find out who I was.

Finally, I discovered Donald (Darden) Johnson after I searched for my identity and security for many years. I was created wonderfully and fearfully in God's image, and God created me to glorify him, be a recipient of his grace, and to be reconciled (restored to a right relationship and fellowship) with him. I discovered who I am through God's plan of salvation, and by accepting Jesus Christ as my Lord and Savior, I learned that I am a child of God!

"For you formed my inward parts; you knitted me together in my mother's womb. I praise you for I am fearfully and wonderfully made. Wonderful are your works; my soul knows it very well. My frame was not hidden from you when I was made in secret, intricately woven in the depths of the earth. Your eyes saw my unformed substance; in your book were written every one of them, the days that were formed for me, when as yet there was none of them" *(Psalm 139:13-16).*

2

Chosen

My identity was problematic early on. I struggled mentally and emotionally as I tried to assert my identity as Donald (Darden) Johnson. I began to understand that an adopted child has his or her unique problems with identity and assimilation.

My adoption was arranged before I was born. My biological mother arranged for her landlords, Lee and Lucille Johnson, to adopt me. The Johnsons brought me home from the hospital after I was born. Lee and Lucille oversaw the property where my birth mother lived during her pregnancy with me. Shortly after my birth, my birth mother moved from the Johnsons' home, she married and gave birth to my three younger half-siblings: Irving, Donna, and Beverly.

Praise God! I always knew who my birth mother was, although there had not been any physical or emotional bond between the two of us. I acknowledged the Johnsons as my only parents for quite a long time, however. The Johnsons never concealed the adoption from me, and we discussed the arrangement for as long as I could remember. The topic came up often because I had a lot of questions about both the adoption and my biological family. My biggest question was, *Why?* It was essential for me to understand *why* I was adopted.

Frequently, my adoptive parents told me that my mother's economic situation prevented her from raising some of her children. My parents would simply say, "She (my birth mother) could not afford to raise or keep you." My three older half-siblings were also adopted. Other family members (especially the biological ones) told me the same thing, and they added that I should be grateful that my birth mother *"brought me into this world"* rather than aborting me. I tried to accept those reasons for my adoption, but it didn't cancel the hurt and disappointment I felt.

I understood the facts, but it didn't explain the "why." None of the truth took away the longing I had to be with my birth family. If only I could rewind my life and decide for myself, I would have chosen to live with my birth mother, despite her economic hardships and other social circumstances. I wouldn't care if there was not enough money, it would just be great to grow up with a bunch of brothers and sisters anyhow. The most important thing would be that we'd live together as a family. I didn't understand the psychological ramifications of being adopted, but I realized the outcomes. It meant that I wouldn't grow up with the nurture and supervision of my birth mother and the companionship of my biological siblings. I felt deprived of my family and identity.

I visited my biological family somewhat often, and we had a good relationship. But something was different. I felt like an outsider when I visited them because I knew each visit to my mom's and stepfather's home was temporary. Every time I left their house, I imagined what it would be like to live with them full-time. That's what I wanted and hoped for. *Why* couldn't we all live happily together? I couldn't understand it. So, the *why* question haunted me.

Loneliness, rejection, depression, and alienation became my closest friends. It seemed no one really understood how I felt. I struggled to belong and be accepted. However, I didn't know that God had a sovereign plan, and he was in control of my life all the time. I was "chosen."

My birth mother chose to birth me, and the Johnsons elected to raise me as their child. God chose me to be a part of his creation, and to experience his amazing grace and love! He appointed me for adoption into his marvelous Kingdom. I realized that being adopted was not a bad thing, after all. It was "a God thing." It was a blessing to be chosen!

"Blessed the God and Father of our Lord Jesus Christ, who has blessed us in Christ with every spiritual blessing in heavenly places..In love, he predestined us for adoption as sons through Jesus Christ, according to the purpose of his will, to the praise of his glorious grace, with which he has blessed us in the Beloved"
(Ephesians 1:3–6).

3

The Transfer

I took the public bus to high school from Mount Victory's south side to the city's north side. The bus fare was about fifteen cents, and the small diesel-powered, unairconditioned public bus was always crowded. My journey required that I take two buses, in which I transferred from one bus to another in order to complete the trip. I resented the daily tiresome trip because it would have been easier if there was a direct route from my community to the high school. But to travel from one point to another has often involved "transfers," whether on a bus, train, plane, or in another life circumstance. Similarly, adoption involved a transfer of a child's legal status.

In a narrow sense, adoption has meant the legal transaction of a child, in which the parental rights of the biological parent are entirely and permanently severed. The legal process included the provision of resources to either birth parent or child, the consolidation of property holdings affected by adopting a child(s), and or a solution to infertility. Adoption involved taking a person (usually a child) into one's own family by a legal process and raising the person as one's own. The process changed the way society views kinship, family, childhood, and personhood. [3]

Even when the transaction is confidential, as it has been in the United States since the early 20th century, adoption exposed fundamental ideas about identity, the normative organization of lives, and adulthood. In a sense, adoption has always been public since the transfer is acknowledged legally. Many times, though, it may be considered "closed" to protect the birth family and the child.[4] The bible recorded some transfers of children in ancient times.

Moses, the deliverer (liberator) of the Hebrew people from Egyptian slavery, was adopted by Pharaoh's daughter (sister). Pharaoh's sister raised him as her child. The Bible put it like this, "…Now the daughter of Pharaoh came down to bathe at the river, while her young women walked beside the river. She saw the basket among the reeds. When she opened it, she saw the child. She took pity on him and said, 'This is one of the Hebrews' children…When the child grew up, she brought him to Pharaoh's daughter, and he became her son" (Exodus 2:1-10).

God had a significant plan for Moses' life, which included his adoption by Pharaoh's sister. Moses' adoption catalyzed God's plan to release his people (Exodus 3:7, 10). God's grace was amazing.

Queen Esther, another person mentioned in the Bible, was an adoptee too. As an orphan, she was adopted by her elder cousin Mordecai. Mordecai continued to look after Esther after she was taken providentially and graciously into the king's palace. God placed her in the right place (the Persian Kingdom) for His ordained purpose, which involved the preservation and deliverance of the Hebrew people. Esther became a national hero despite her identity conflicts.

One commentator said it like this, "The heroine Esther is a developing character...She has two names hinting at the identity crisis that she undergoes when she rises to the highest level of Persian society. But Esther becomes heroic by the ordeal of needing to save her nation."[5] The Jews were spared political extermination because of her faith, courage, and divine "positioning" by God. Esther was called to trust in God's providence for the protection and liberation of her people. Her example has taught people of faith to live with courage and integrity despite our backgrounds and circumstances. God has a purpose for our lives.

Jesus was conceived by the Holy Ghost in his mother Mary's womb. Joseph, to whom Mary was engaged, adopted Christ as his legal son. "When his mother Mary had been betrothed to Joseph before they came together she was found to be with child from the Holy Spirit...an angel of the Lord appeared to him in a dream saying, Joseph, son of David, do not fear to take Mary as your wife...She will bear a son, and you shall call his name Jesus" (Matthew 1:11-21). Joseph became Jesus' legal earthly father. The transfers of children (adoption) span not only human history but God's plans also.

Ultimately, it was Jesus' death, burial, and resurrection that provided the means for people to be adopted into God's heavenly family. The Apostle Paul writing to the churches in the regions of Galatia explained it this way, "But when the fullness of time had come, God sent forth his Son, born of a woman, born under the law, to redeem those who were under the law so that we might receive adoption as sons" (Galatians 4:4-5). Jesus paid our transfer fee with his blood at Calvary's cross. We become adopted children of God, a legal heir of his rights and benefits, and joint-heirs with Jesus Christ when we are born again (John 1:11-12 and 3:7, Romans 8:14-17, 1 John 3:1). In other words, God transfers us from darkness into his marvelous light!

"Giving thanks to the Father, who has qualified you to share in the inheritance of the saints in light. He has delivered us from the domain of darkness and transferred us to the Kingdom of his beloved Son, in whom we have redemption, the forgiveness of sins" (Colossians 1:12-14).

4

Ashamed

The word *'adoption'* has generated distorted pictures of children, families, and societies throughout the ages. It has evoked images of sallow and pallid children or abandoned infants left to die in their birth hospital. Others have pictured groups of misguided children living in abject poverty and overseen by gruesome caretakers. In the past, many believed a society that fostered adoptive care was promoting immoral behavior in the unmarried mothers' lives.[6] To some extent, similar attitudes have persisted.

Most people responded with surprise or sympathy when I told them I was adopted. Nonverbally, they seemed to say, "Oh, poor you!" For a long time, I agreed with them. I grew up with the sociological and psychological understanding that being 'adopted' was a deviation from the cultural norms. Reports indicated more than ninety-seven percent of adopted children know they were adopted, and most children (nine out of ten) feel positive about their situation.[7] But many adoptees have encountered challenges at different points in their lives.

Feelings of loss, grief, low self-esteem, and formation identity issues have been familiar with adopted children while they grew up. We felt grief, anxiety, anger, and the loss of birthparents, siblings, and family culture. These emotions aroused feelings of uncertainty and doubt. Adopted children have wondered, *What's wrong with me? Will my adoptive parents leave me also?* Identity development that began in childhood becomes increasingly prominent throughout the teenage years.[8]

In adolescence, children started to explore and understand who they are, where they came from, and their purpose in life. For adopted children, filling in the blanks has created an extra challenge. They have perceived themselves to be different, out-of-place, or unwelcome in social circles. They have felt they did not fit in with others. This lack of confidence was most perceptible in children who felt embarrassed or ashamed of their adoption.[9] Adoption was a tremendous emotional roller coaster ride for me. It affected the way I viewed myself and how I related to other people.

James Garbarino has been hailed as a pioneer in helping us understand youths. He did extensive work with children and violence, and he conveyed an analysis after observing abandoned teenagers in moments of their intense sadness. He reported that social barriers or psychological issues that prevent considerable healthy, competent, and caring parenting causes a breakdown in child development. "And when his earliest parent-child relationship doesn't take hold and thrive, a boy is left emotionally high and dry. What shame a boy feels as his mother abandons him."[10] Mr. Garabino's investigation has been validated in many instances and across demographics.

Fortunately, however, God has always been sovereignly in control of peoples' lives and situations. His grace has rescued and healed many lost boys and souls. God has been a father to the fatherless and a judge of widows. His grace made it possible for me to survive and thrive! I came this far by grace. Thank you, Jesus.

"For you did not receive the spirit of slavery to fall back into fear, but you have received the Spirit of adoption as sons, by whom we cry, Abba Father!"
(Romans 8:15).

5

A Time to be Born

"For everything, there is a season, and a time for every matter under heaven: a time to be born, and a time to die" (*Ecclesiastes 3:1-2*).

I was born in 1954 in an era of transition. A case named Brown vs. the Board of Education came before the Supreme Court that year, and the petitioners argued that segregation in public facilities was unconstitutional. The court unanimously agreed. The landmark civil rights decision authored by Thurgood Marshall marked the legalized end of the segregated stronghold in the American South. The civil rights movement took off.[11] The mid-1950s gave rise to many other transformations also.

The Salk vaccine, developed by Jonas Salk, was administered for the first time in 1954. The vaccine defended children against polio, and cases decreased from 14,647 to 5,894 in the United States by 1956.[12] Medical and scientific discoveries improved rapidly and changed the world. Also, in 1954, Marilyn Monroe, the legendary

Hollywood actress, married Joe DiMaggio, the famous baseball player. As well, the words *"under God"* were added to the pledge of allegiance that year. It didn't make media headlines, but I was born the same year also.

I was born in a small suburban city named Mount Victory, located just north of the Bronx, New York. What was once a small town had grown to almost 75,000 people by the time I was born. Mount Victory became one of the most densely populated cities in America as people moved there in pursuit of economic opportunity, suburbia, and the American dream.

Many of my relatives moved to Mount Victory during the Great American Migration. They joined six million other African Americans who migrated from the rural south to urban cities in Northeast, Midwest, and Western America. My maternal grandparents moved from Tennessee to Kentucky and settled in West Virginia eventually. My adoptive parents moved from Mississippi to the north, probably in the early 1940s, and they ended up living in Mount Victory. Mount Victory was a great place to be born and raised.

I thrived as a youth in my hometown, and I was involved in school, church, and the community that I loved. I didn't understand or really appreciate it when I grew up, but I was born in the right place and at the right time. Everything I experienced in my youth and young adult life, it prepared me to become who I am and how I serve Jesus Christ today. Amazing grace!

What was true for me is true for you also. God planned the birth and circumstances of our lives before we were born. He knew the time and place where we'd be born, our parents, and the purposes our lives would serve. He does not make mistakes. Like the seasons, God's timing has always been perfect and purposeful. Hallelujah!

> *"While the earth remains, seedtime and harvest, cold and heat, summer and winter, day and night shall not cease. And God blessed Noah and his sons and said to them, 'Be fruitful and multiply and fill the earth"*
> *(Genesis 8:22–9:1).*

6

A Prophecy

Shortly after I entered the church fellowship hall, I'd hear, *"God is omniscient; he is omnipotent; and he is omnipresent. Omniscient-means God is all-knowing; Omnipotent-that means God is all-powerful; and Omnipresent-God is present everywhere at all times,"* Deacon Jones said every Wednesday evening in Bible class. Then, he'd smile broadly, and wait for an "Amen" or two from the class members. Deacon Jones was our Bible teacher. A prominent church deacon, and a well-respected community member, he was a godly example to me for many years. I learned and remembered the attributes of God when I was a child.

I loved the church since I first attended when I was four years old. I never forgot how I was mesmerized by the pastor's appearance and how his countenance captivated me. Pastor Nelson's face looked like an angel's, and he had "a mysterious" visible glow around him. That young, I knew the church was a special place with special people-God's people!

I was mandated by my grandfather to attend Sunday School,

but my attending the afternoon church service was optional. But soon Sunday School, the church service, and Wednesday night Bible classes were a part of my life. I was one of the youngest people in the Wednesday night Bible class.

One night, after Bible class, Deacon Jones asked me to be the "junior speaker" the following Wednesday. Nervously, I agreed, although I was clueless about what I should do. I had a book of Bible stories at home. One of the stories was about the Exodus, the rescue of the Hebrews from Egyptian slavery. The narrative included The Ten Commandments also.

The Ten Commandments were my favorite to read, and I understood them better than the other Bible stories. I had started to memorize the Ten Commandments, so I decided to speak about them the following Wednesday in Bible class. Naturally, all experienced preachers would have developed an introduction, three points, and a conclusion to their sermon, but I simply wrote on a piece of paper each commandment and prepared to read them. That was the short and long preparation for my first "public sermon." But I rehearsed it regularly.

I wanted to read The Ten Commandments as best I could. The next Wednesday came, and I stood to read. I became a little excited, and I was even more surprised when everyone applauded after I finished reading. It was something I did not forget. Deacon Jones, our instructor, was elated, and he brimmed with joy. As soon as I finished speaking, he ran to me, and excitedly said, "You're gonna be a preacher."

I sighed within. I was less than exuberant about what Deacon Jones said. I had hoped he wouldn't say that to me. Silently, I downplayed his prediction and thought, *"Oh no, I am not! I am* *not going to be a preacher or anything of the sort. **I** have other plans for my life and career. And, it does not include being a preacher."*

For many years, I tried to ignore what Deacon Jones said, but later I found myself hiding in rebellion, drug addiction, alcoholism, and immorality to avoid surrendering my life and will to Jesus Christ. Eventually, I accepted God's plan for my life and destiny, and Deacon Jones' prophesy became a reality. Not only did I get saved, born-again, but I became a preacher also. I couldn't deny or ignore God's plan any longer. His sovereignty and love won hands down!

"Before I formed you in the womb, I knew you, and before you were born, I consecrated you; I appointed you a prophet to the nations"
(Jeremiah 1:5).

7

We Are Family!

We Are Family hit the airwaves in 1979 with the signature song and album produced by the R & B group Sister Sledge. In my neighborhood, the song boomed from our cheap stereo record players all the time. But for some of us, the song's lyrics carried a mixed message. After all, my family life was complicated, unlike the happy-go-lucky theme in the song. I really wished, *"I had all my brothers and sisters with me,"* as the song said!

I was born to a single, young mother (age 21), who had three older children. My mother migrated to New York from a small coal-mining town in West Virginia. My grandparents reared her in an intact God-fearing household, and her father, a church deacon, worked as a coal miner. My grandmother (Grandma Fredina) was a stay-at-home mom and the church mother of Mt. Nebo Baptist Church in Claremont, West Virginia. My mother's early life, like mine, was complicated.

When I talked to her about her life growing up, my mother conceded she had low self-esteem as the middle child of ten children. She believed she was "ugly." Her beliefs led to her having a poor self-image and negative feelings, something which, without any intervention, she did not outgrow. She dropped out of school early, and when she was about fourteen years old, she gave birth to my oldest sibling. I was the fourth child born to her before she married.

Due to her different circumstances, my mother placed her older children for adoption. But praise be to God, she sought good homes for her children despite her inability to raise them. I was placed in a loving and caring home, and I was blessed with God-fearing parents.

My adoptive parents Lee and Lucille Johnson were beautiful people. It seemed my adoptive mother, Lucille, possessed a fountain of unconditional love. I loved her with all my being, and undoubtedly, I was a "momma's boy." The Johnsons raised me from my birth, and I became their legal child when I was about six years old. I felt accepted by my immediate and extended adoptive family, and I never remembered my family telling me, "You were adopted." The adoption arrangement was especially welcomed by Lucille because she had longed to raise a child of her own.

Lucille became pregnant with her first child when she was only twelve years old. She and her firstborn (a son) were almost like 'sister and brother' as they both continued to be raised by Lucille's mother. Lucille married her first husband when she was fourteen, and after the marriage, she birthed her second child, a daughter. The child died from rheumatic fever about two years post her birth. Lucille longed to raise children, but she found herself deprived of motherhood when she was just sixteen years old.

Both my adoptive parents, Lucille and Lee Johnson, were born in the Mississippi delta region. They married in their adult lives in Pine Bluff, Arkansas, and the couple moved to New York sometime in the early 1940s. After living in the city for a while, the couple tried to adopt my one-year older sister, Doll, but the adoption fell through. After my conception, when my birth mother conceded she would place me for adoption too, Lucille was anxious to adopt me. It was an opportunity for her and her husband, Lee, to realize their dream of raising a child. The Johnsons brought me to their home from my birth hospital, and we became a family!

> "Sing to God, sing praises to his name; lift up a song to
> him who rides through the deserts; his name is the LORD...
> Father of the fatherless and protector of widows is God in
> his holy habitation. God settles the solitary in a home"
> (Psalm 68:4-6).

8

Words Have Power

The expression "sticks and stones may break my bones, but names will never hurt me" has been said often. But it is only partially true. Yes, sticks and stones have broken many bones, but harmful *names* have hurt too. Names have bruised, injured, embarrassed, isolated, and made people feel inferior. Throughout my life, I experienced the powerful denigration of being called "names."

It took some time before I trusted people to get my legal name correct after my early childhood experiences. But everything smoothed out eventually. By the first grade and our relocation to live in public housing, most everyone called me *Donald Johnson*. But then, I faced a new identity challenge and "name-calling." The other children often taunted me.

I felt different from the very beginning, and I was conflicted about my identity in different ways. I started to struggle with my gender when I was very young, and I appeared effeminate to others and myself. I felt uncomfortable with my mannerisms, both in public and private. I vividly remembered when I started to feel terrible about what people said about me.

My adoptive mother was friends with a couple of gay males who visited our home sometimes. One guy named Teddy, after several beers, was filled with ridicule. He teased my mother about my effeminate mannerisms and high-pitched voice. My mother just tried to downplay Teddy's taunts. But I understood his innuendos as I grew older. Teddy intimated that my early childhood effeminacy was an indication of me being gay. He never "called me names," but he certainly made fun of me. His accusations left an impression.

Sometimes I believed Teddy was right. I wasn't sure. I hadn't questioned my sexuality, and I hadn't thought about my future lifestyle, either. I was still a child. The next painful incident took place two years later.

Our family didn't own a washing machine, so we used the community laundromat in the project's building next to where my grandparents lived. I loved going to the semi-hidden basement laundry room with Mama Lucille. The laundry was a vibrant place in the community where the women washed clothes and shared their gossip. On one occasion, I overheard a conversation my mother was having with another lady in the laundry.

"*Donnie's going to be one*," my mother said. (Donnie was my nickname). I couldn't believe what my mother said to the other woman. I tried to act like I didn't hear it as I ate a bag of potato chips and drank a five cents cola from Uncle Willies' store. I became silent.

"*Donnie's going to be one*." The words repeatedly rang in my ears. I tried to deny what my mother said, but I heard her speak for myself, and I knew what she meant. I felt betrayed. She took Teddy's jokes about me and my identity seriously. Ma believed her friend Teddy, "*a warped expert in my childhood development,*" more than she believed in me. Ma's words bothered me a long time, and her words had an influence over my life and destiny.

Herein is a word of caution to parents, caregivers, educators, youth leaders, pastors, etcetera. A lesson is to be learned through my experience. Words have power.

The things we say to our children can either give life to them or destroy them. I suggest strongly that you intentionally speak words of grace, love, favor, and holiness in your children's lives. Don't just nurture and love them but understand and know them also. Be convinced that God created us all in his image and likeness and that children are an inheritance from the Lord (Psalm 127:3).

Children are a gift despite the circumstances from which they were born. We may see our children from our perspectives, but God views them from his. Train a child in the way he or she should go; even when they are old, they will not depart from it (Proverbs 22:6). Speak God's words over their lives, and into their minds and hearts. "Faith comes from hearing and hearing through the word of Christ" (Romans 10:17). Words can be self-fulfilling prophecies.

Throughout life, I've learned to ignore and overcome negative things. I learned to believe God's words rather than peoples' comments about me. I didn't know God orchestrated my life before I was born, and that he had a plan. It took more than three decades before I trusted God's Word and discovered his purpose for my life. It was a journey out of darkness into God's marvelous light, and I thank him for his amazing grace!

"For those whom he foreknew, he also predestined
to be conformed to the image of his Son"
(Romans 8:29).

9

Sex?

I heard about sexual activity at some point in childhood, but the topic was not discussed in my home. Sex was a mystery to me, and I assumed my parents were too elderly for the activity. The topic of sex was not only taboo, but I thought it might have been strange or even perverse when I grew up. Sex has been one of the most misunderstood acts in life.

Often naively, sex has been relegated to one's device and imagination. Sex, however, has been defined in either of two ways: (1.) as a distinction between male and female gender; and (2.) that in which persons, plants, or animals are distinct regarding their reproductive functions.[13] The Bible recognized sex in both categories. "So, God created man in his image; in the image of God, he created him, male and female, he created them. And God blessed them, and God said to them be fruitful and multiply and fill the earth and subdue it, and have dominion over the fish of the sea, the birds of the heavens, and over every living thing that moves upon the earth" (Genesis 1:27-28).

God identified sex not only as an instrument of human distinction, but for procreation, and earth stewardship. Sex was involved in the Creation. "And God said, Let the waters swarm with swarms of living creatures, and let birds fly above the earth across the expanse of the heavens. So, God created the great sea creatures and every living creature that moves. And God blessed them saying, Be fruitful and multiply and fill the waters in the seas, and let birds multiply in the earth" (Genesis 1:20-22). As well, intimate propagation played an essential role in establishing a human civilization on earth.

> But for Adam, there was not found a helper fit for him. So, the LORD God caused a deep sleep to fall upon the man, and while he slept, took one of his ribs and closed its place with flesh. And the rib that the Lord God had taken from the man he made into (built) a woman and brought her to the man. The man called his wife's name, Eve. Now Adam knew Eve, his wife, and she conceived and bore Cain, saying I have gotten a man with the help of the LORD. And again, she bore his brother Abel" (Genesis 2:20-22, 3:20, 4:1-2).

Adam and Eve illustrated that God's plan for sex is productive. So again, what was the purpose of sex in humanity's beginnings? Dr. Tony Evans explained it well in one of his Kingdom marriages teaching series.

Dr. Evans indicated that sex is an emblem of the biblical

marriage covenant between a man and a woman. All the covenants in The Bible involved God and people, as each party agreed to fulfill an obligation when the bond was established. Typically, a biblical contract was endorsed (signed) with blood.

Dr. Evans highlighted that blood is shed when a marriage covenant is completed or consummated, and the man and woman become one in God's sight. They have covenanted their love and fidelity to each other and agreed to love one another until they depart by human death. The marriage covenant was consummated (fulfilled) by sexual intercourse.

Russell Moore stated in his book, *The Storm-Tossed Family, How the Cross Reshapes the Home*, that since humanity's fall thousands of years ago, people have misinterpreted sex in that we either trivialize or worship it. Many people will have multiple sexual partners throughout their lifetimes in our society, and some have spent their entire lives chasing the mirage of an utterly transcendent sexual experience. Often, the Bible spoke of sexuality and idolatry in tandem throughout the Old and the New Testaments.

Moore added, "A Christian vision of sexuality is neither of these things. But in a universe under the occupation of unseen rulers, we should not be surprised to see sexuality unhinged from the Gospel. Moore stressed that in an era "obsessed with sexuality," the Christian message "must inevitably speak of how it differs from the spirit of the age."

Sexual intercourse, in a Christian rendering, is a reiteration of the union, a renewing of vows, Moore wrote. "As a couple clings to one another in this way, it signals once again that they belong to each other. It is a sign of the Gospel."[14] Sex, according to God's plan and design, has been clarified as being beautiful!

> *"And God saw everything that he had made,*
> *and behold it was very good"*
> *(Genesis 1:31).*

10

🔥

Curiosity Killed the Cat, Grace and Truth Brought Him Back

I was a probing and inquisitive youngster growing up. Sometimes my curiosity was hilarious, and people would say, "*Donald, curiosity killed the cat...*" My friends and elders implied that pursuing answers to one's questions can be detrimental, but with the sublime, I'd reply, "*Yes, curiosity killed the cat, but satisfaction brought him back.*" I wanted to understand myself, life, family, and the world.

I found myself increasingly curious about sex. My parents were very inconspicuous in their married sex lives, and they forbade my involvement in any sexual activity in my youth, but I remained curious. I believed I needed to learn what I was ignorant of.

I wasn't sure why sexual inquisitiveness took hold at such an early age, but I became more interested as I grew older. What was the catalyst for my curiosity? Hormonal changes, physiological drives, peer pressure, the absence of my biological parents, a fallen nature? I didn't know. Later, I decided to explore it for myself.

I started having sexual inclinations in the first or second grade, and I began experimenting with sex when I was age nine or ten. My proclivities led from one thing to another, and then I started to engage in sexual experimentations regularly with an older boy. I also started seeking self-pleasure, and I acquired my first known addiction when I was about ten or eleven years old. Soon, I developed a powerful same-sex attraction, and I attained an identity that frightened me. Sexual promiscuity became normal.

Unfortunately, proper perspectives of sex have been convoluted in our society. Many cultures, aspects of the media, entertainment, inappropriate guidance, and sin have perverted the purpose and God's design of sex. The influences have caused many people (and children) to indulge and create ideas about sex in a non-biblical way. But God is good!

God called me out of sinful darkness into His gracious and marvelous light. It took years of intercessory prayer, a spiritual rebirth, the church, family, self-immersed bible study, and the support of other Christians before I overcame and subdued the sexually promiscuous lifestyle I developed as a child. But it is possible to be an overcomer! I made a willful decision to no longer seek my pleasure. Instead, I surrendered my life to God and indulged in the things that please him. I have not regretted my decision at all.

"The body is not meant for sexual immorality, but for the Lord, and the Lord for the body..Flee from sexual immorality. Every other sin a person commits is outside the body, but the sexually immoral person sins against his own body"
(1 Corinthians 6:13,18).

11

Misfit

John's Bargain Stores were a popular low-end retail store in the 1960s. The stores' names highlighted the word "bargain" with their giant red and white letters. By the mid-1960s, there were 527 John's Bargain Stores in the New York Metropolitan area located primarily in southern New York. [15]

There was a John's Bargain Store in my neighborhood. A step-above today's famous Dollar General Store, John's Bargain, was a "godsend" for my family as we struggled financially. Both my parents and I could afford to shop there as often as we liked for the most part.

One year, I purchased a pair of sneakers in John's Bargain Store for my sixth grade gym class. There was only one pair of sneakers in the store that even remotely fit me, and they were too small. But I bought the sneakers because they were affordable. For an entire school year, I crammed my feet into that pair of ill-fitted sneakers. Eventually, I had to admit the shoes were a "misfit" after my toes suffered some permanent damage.

I never forgot the experience I had with those sneakers, and I felt stupid for buying them. However, the ordeal made me reflect on how I felt about myself growing up. I felt like a misfit.

I hated gym class, and I was not athletically gifted like most kids in my community. I felt unsuited for masculine and physically challenging sports, and it seemed like I didn't measure up to other boys. I was uncomfortable around them. Most of my close friends were with girls, but of course, I didn't entirely fit in with them either. I was ostracized, and I felt like a misfit.

I was confused about my gender, family, and surroundings, and I longed for genuine acceptance. I was popular in school and had friends, but I still felt like an oddball. I lived a lonely and emotionally isolated life. Then, one day I became born again, saved, Hallelujah!

Finally, I realized there is a place in God's Kingdom for everyone who repents and believes in Jesus Christ. There are no *misfits.* Jesus' sacrificial death, resurrection, and atonement for our sins made it possible for everyone to become a citizen in the Kingdom of God. I began to identify myself as God's son, his accepted and redeemed child. Thank God for his amazing grace!

"Let not your hearts be troubled. Believe in God; believe also in me. In my Father's house are many rooms. If it were not so, would I have told you that I go to prepare a place for you? And if I go and prepare a place for you, I will come again and take you to myself, that where I am you may be also"
(John 14:1-3).

12

The Prince and The Pauper

Mark Twain was known as the father of American literature, and he wrote more than eighteen books. He wrote the novel 'The Prince and the Pauper' in 1882. The story involved two main characters, a pauper named Tom Canty; and the Prince of Wales, whose name was Edward Tudor. The fictional tale took place in sixteenth-century London, England.

The story began as follows, "In the ancient city of London, on a certain autumn day, in the second quarter of the sixteenth century, a boy (Tom Canty) was born to a poor family of the name Canty who did not want him. On the same day, another English child (Prince Edward) was born to a wealthy family of the name of Tudor, who did want him." Twain added, "(Prince Edward) lay lapped in silks and satins. But there was no talk about the other baby, Tom Canty, lapped in his poor rags, except among the family of paupers whom he had just come to trouble with his presence."

Tom Canty, raised in a depressed household and environment, grew up poor. At first, he accepted his degenerate lot in life, but later, he became unhappy with his inauspicious circumstances. Tom dreamed of being a prince as a local priest tutored him. Tom started acting like a prince even. Then, one day his dream came true.

Tom Canty met Prince Edward. The boys talked, and they became fascinated with each other's life. Ingeniously, they decided to trade places with each other. Prince Edward attired himself with Tom's clothing, and soon after, the Prince of Wales was expelled from the royal palace. Tom took Edward's place in the castle, but the boys' role reversals confused the royal court.

Tom Canty, unused to royal splendor, would bow to the court officials at times the officers were supposed to bow to him. He didn't adjust quickly to the princely lifestyle, and Edward, the true prince, experienced an audacious life as he lived vicariously as a pauper.[16] Mark Twain wrote the legendary novel with artful realism.

I related to the story entirely. Sometimes I felt a little bit like a prince, other times like a pauper when I grew up. I loved acting the role of a prince much more than that of a pauper, however.

I played the role of the prince in our elementary school's French production of Cinderella. Mrs. Iron, our French teacher, produced and directed a significant school production in French every year. Everyone knew the Cinderella production was Mrs. Iron's signature statement in the Language Arts Department. It was legendary! Mrs. Iron's second-year French students made up the production cast.

I could hardly focus on my first year of French class as I anticipated being in next year's drama production. I hoped to have a supporting role in the play, at least. I was also aware that either

Aaron Wells or myself might have a leading role since we were some of the few males in the class. I loved the French language, and it was one of my favorite subjects. The time came for the auditions shortly after we began the sixth-grade Fall term.

I thought about the production day and night, and I rehearsed a lot. I memorized the entire script for the part of the prince. I had seen the play performed before by my older schoolmates, and I knew I had to exhibit my best acting (and French-speaking) abilities for a lead role. I was anxious, but the auditions went smoother than I thought. Mrs. Iron made the decisions after one or two acting tryouts. She announced in the school auditorium, "Tia Gray will play the part of Cinderella. Donald Johnson will be the prince." Six months later, the production was on.

The day of the drama came, and excitement permeated the entire atmosphere. The production went like clockwork, and every actor and tech person were at their best. The play was magnificent! The show climaxed with the legendary surprise, Cinderella, of all people, came gallantly to the ball, and she received the hand of Prince Charming. The play ended as Princess Cinderella (Tia Gray), and I (Prince Charming) joined hands and smiled. The stage curtains closed, and then quickly, the curtains were raised again!

The sixth-grade actors stepped forward to take a bow as the audience applauded robustly with a standing ovation! I was elated as I glanced over the school auditorium filled with enthusiastic classmates, teachers, and parents. But suddenly, I noticed one thing- neither of my parents or any of my family members were in the auditorium. A wave of sadness ran over me as I fought back my disappointment just before I took my bow. I bowed, and the curtains closed again.

Backstage, I realized my parents hadn't been present for most of the events I was involved in, not even my church baptism. Mom and Dad didn't attend church when I grew up, so I had to excuse them for not being at the youth events I led and organized. Lack of money was an issue for our family also, so in all fairness, I could not expect them to take time off from work for my school plays or church events. But our sixth-grade production of Cinderella was different.

Mrs. Iron, Tia Gray, the other students, and me, we worked hard to continue the Language Arts legacy in our school. A bit of history was being preserved, and we wanted our loved ones to witness it! More importantly, for me, it was an occasion when I, who felt like a pauper, got to act like a "prince."

My parents' lack of participation and support in my school and church activities bothered me a lot. They didn't know it, but their non-involvement enhanced my identity struggles. But all praise to God when I accepted Jesus Christ as my Lord and Savior, my identity crisis was resolved. I became "a King's kid," and God's grace made me both royal and humble.

*"For my father and my mother have forsaken
me, but the Lord will take me in"
(Psalm 27:11).*

13

A Teenage Rebel

It was a cold, breezy, and cloudy afternoon in late October. Reluctantly, I walked with both my adoptive parents into the small waiting room in the Board of Education on the city's north side. We sat in the vestibule for a few minutes, and then a secretary whisked us down the hallway into a sterile-looking rectangular room with white walls. The school psychologist, at first sitting behind a desk, stood up, and greeted my parents and me as we walked into the room. "Hi, I'm the school psychologist," she said. My parents said hello, but I did not reply. I couldn't believe my parents followed through with my sixth-grade teacher's referral.

It was early in my sixth year of school when my teacher and school officials referred me to the psychologist. I hated the ordeal, and I was angry. I was upset mostly with my sixth-grade teacher, Miss Leila Jackson, who recommended the intervention.

Miss Jackson was a slender, young, Caucasian woman, a native of Mississippi. She had migrated to New York, but she maintained her southern values. Miss Jackson worked in the school one year before becoming my homeroom and primary teacher. She was a hard worker charged with educating some troublesome pupils. Most of the students were African American and urban youths, some of which were headed for trouble already. Miss Jackson singled me out.

My behavior was "off the charts" in Miss Jackson's class, and I disrespected her. I made fun of her southern accent, as did most of the other kids in our class. She had a reputation for not having much control over her classroom. Miss Jackson was concerned not only with my incorrigibility, but she took notice of my increasing effeminate behavior also. By the sixth grade, I had become diminutively masculine as I associated mostly with girls and adopted an effeminate lifestyle. She intervened by arranging a meeting with my parents.

Miss Jackson advised my parents of her apprehension about my academic future. She indicated I was a high achiever, but that my success was in jeopardy because of peer influences and identity conflicts. She recommended that I attend junior high school on the north side instead of in my community. It was decided in the meeting that I would be bussed to the city's northside junior high school with me starting the seventh grade. I was stunned. My friends and I had waited for six long years to go to junior high school together. Suddenly, the plan was down the tubes.

I didn't understand why or appreciate that I had to visit the psychologist and attend junior high school in another community. I felt like I was being imprisoned emotionally. I decided during my first appointment with the psychologist, that if I had anything to do with it, it would be my last visit. Manipulatively, I discussed the way I felt with my parents.

I asked them why other people had to be involved in my life? I used "self-pity," and I told them I had suffered enough from being adopted. I tried to persuade my parents that I didn't need to change, and if I did, it was going to be complicated, maybe too difficult for me to achieve. I talked my parents into seeing things my way, and they decided we wouldn't seek any additional psychological intervention. Later I believed my parents' lack of resolve in the interventions helped to fuel my rebellion.

I grew to dislike my adoptive father. I felt deprived of his paternal affirmation and love. He was physically present, and he provided for our household, but I perceived him to be emotionally "absent" in my life in some ways. I rebelled, and my history of sexual promiscuity was an indication of my resentment and emotional deprivation.

> "I call heaven and earth to witness against you today, that
> I have set before you life and death, blessing and curse.
> Therefore choose life, that you and your offspring may live,
> loving the LORD your God, obeying his voice, and holding fast
> to him, for he is your life and length of days, that you may
> dwell in the land that the LORD swore to your fathers..."
> (Deuteronomy 30:19–20).

14

Objection!

The 1960s ushered massive advances in America and the world. Many changes hurled from the civil rights movement that began in 1954[17] as the movement gained momentum. In 1964, three civil rights workers were killed in Mississippi that summer, and the same year, former President Lyndon B. Johnson signed the Civil Rights Acts Bill into law ending segregation in employment and education in America. Shortly after, The War on Poverty was declared.[18] Society heaved upwards in reforms.

The Vietnam War escalated, and social protests and riots globalized. Pictures of starving Biafran children took front and center during a civil war in Nigeria. The world realized a new consciousness amidst the cultural changes, and the counterculture movement took the world by a storm.

Anti-war protesters, supporters and antagonists of civil rights, the emerging media, and the rejection of mainstream religion, all contributed to a counter-culture movement that originated in Europe.[19] A new era in music and entertainment began as contemporary rock and roll groups like The Beatles took center stage. The sexual revolution was a significant but problematic part of counter-culturalism.

The sexual revolution countered the traditional codes of sexuality and interpersonal relationships. It normalized premarital sex, homosexuality, public nudity, and alternate forms of sexuality. The anarchy led to the legalization of the pill, other contraception, and abortion.[20] Life changed in America and the western world as things progressed. A new era dawned.

I thought it was great to be a teenager during the time, and soon I found myself a part of the new culture. I became a teenage revolutionist, and foolishly opposed the traditional codes of behavior and morality. I regretted my choices later.

> *"Does not wisdom call? Does not understanding raise her voice? On the heights beside the way, at the crossroads she takes her stand; beside the gates in front of the town... To you, O men, I call, and my cry is to the children of man. O simple ones learn prudence; O fools learn sense"*
> *(Proverbs 8:1–5).*

15

"Partners"

"No temptation has overtaken you that is not common to man. God is faithful, and he will not let you be tempted beyond your ability, but with the temptation he will also provide the way of escape, that you may be able to endure it"
(1 Corinthians 10:13).

The counter-cultural changes did not occur in isolation during the 1960s to the 1980s. There was an infusion of ambivalence, confusion, and compromise in society. Young adults were significantly challenged as they grew up in two of the most significant events in western history-civil rights and counter-culturalism. Illicit drug use, civil rights boycotts, and protests to the Vietnam War were common. Thankfully, my transition from elementary school to junior high was successful.

Amid this, I resented the fact that I was bussed to the city's north side junior high school. I felt segregated, and I missed my friends. I looked forward to the summer when I'd spend time in my "own community." Meanwhile, a new clothing store named *Partners* opened in our neighborhood.

The store looked trendy from the outside, and its facade resembled the "hippie" stores in New York City's Greenwich Village. Situated on a corner of our two-blocks town shopping center, Partners Store stood out. It was odd.

There was also a strange ambiance inside the dimly lit store, and I smelled incense the first time I went inside. I sensed an aura of suspiciousness. I was not surprised to learn that marijuana was sold inside the store as well as clothing. One of my friend's older brothers worked in the store.

My friend's brother was involved in the emergent drug subculture, and he regularly shared marijuana with his younger brother, DaShaun. DaShaun and I were friends. We lived in the same apartment building.

DaShaun looked like the coolest, hippest, and most grown-up kid in our neighborhood. He had dark thick wavy black hair, and he was fair-skinned. He dressed very well. However, there were several differences between him and me.

DaShaun didn't have a curfew, and seemingly no parental restrictions. He didn't attend school regularly, and more than once, he was committed to the state's residential care. DaShaun didn't attend the same church as my friends and me. The church was an important part of my life since I was four years old. Also, I had a curfew, several limitations imposed by my parents, and I loved going to school. DaShaun and I had very little in common, but he insisted on being my friend. DaShaun was a bully, and he tried to control me.

Bullying was by no means unusual in the tough southside neighborhood I grew up in, but my friend DaShaun earned "a particular reputation." He was a social menace, and he fought with almost everybody he knew. He intimidated me a lot. I was surprised to discover that DaShaun was attending the same northside junior high school I was mandated to attend. I couldn't escape him and his influence.

I had heard about marijuana, but I knew very little about it. DaShaun's brother kept him supplied with the weed, but I had no plans to smoke it. One day, DaShaun gave me some of his marijuana.

It seemed harmless at first. I excused it and said that's what friends are for-we share, we're "partners." Unfortunately, I liked the effects of marijuana almost immediately. It made me feel giddy and act silly. Subconsciously, I became convinced that pot could make me happy, even in my depression, loneliness, and rejection.

I smoked marijuana several more times, and it became the key to making me feel happy. It was my therapy, and I escaped from reality. But it was a deadly self-prescription. Marijuana helped alter my decision making to the point I became accepting and open to use other drugs. I started to use heroin a short while later.

"There is a way that seems right to a man,
but its end is the way to death"
(Proverbs 14:12).

16

Summertime!

New York summers were always hot, and the summer of '68 was no exception. The air was thick with humidity, and the breezes were stifling. From ten blocks away, the subway's fumes perfused the air in our congested southside neighborhood with about six hundred people. Our neighborhood was comprised of five tall concrete public housing buildings, and each structure accommodated one hundred families.

The buildings' structures were as strong as the Hoover Dam, and they withstood almost any outside or inside elements. The complex's flagpole in the middle of the park was the only thing that wavered in the hurricane and blizzard seasons. The community park was in the middle of the five buildings, and it was the center of community activity.

Especially in the summertime, people vacated their unairconditioned apartments to frequent the park because the park was the only place one could catch a cool breeze of wind late at night or early in the morning. The park was also where single mothers and grandmothers convened with their children during the day. The young mothers updated each other about their latest romantic interests, and the grandmothers discussed how the Holy Spirit touched them when they listened to Mahalia Jackson's latest gospel record. The park was our community's safe gathering place. But that changed around 1968.

The scent of water from fire hydrogens, subway fumes, and teenage sweat from the nearby playgrounds became less familiar. Instead, there was a trace of something else. It was a strange ambiance that overwhelmed the park, and one could almost smell what seemed like an artificial perfume. Suddenly, most people stopped frequenting the park.

It was as if there was a sign "Enter at your own risk" at the park's entrance as parents forbade their children and teenagers from resorting to the community arena. We began to see uninvited people roaming in the area, and soon the strangers were identified as "undercover" police officers. Rumors, prohibitions, and secrets escalated in the community as tensions increased. Our community was no longer the open and friendly enclave it used to be.

Regularly I heard neighbors say, *"Did you hear about so and so? They got caught!"* I thought, 'caught?' I imagined someone had had an illicit extramarital affair, or maybe a person stole an item from Johns Bargain Store. Or did someone else get arrested for gambling and writing numbers? I assumed they did. Then, I discovered why people were being "caught." People were arrested for illegal possession of street drugs in our neighborhood, and they went to jail. The environment changed.

Marijuana was being sold in our shopping center, and heroin was available in the community park. The park became the site for heroin users to buy drugs and nod off their intoxication, instead of the place children gathered to play jacks and double-dutch jump rope. Subtly, but obtrusively, the drug craze invaded our territory, and sabotaged our community's vitality. Soon much of our entire city resembled a warzone devastated by the counterculture. The situation was gravely more than I imagined, and an epidemic had begun.

Many people were hooked on drugs in the summer of 1968, and some began an expedition of substance abuse lasting a lifetime while others soon died from heroin overdoses. I finished junior high school just before the summer began, and it was the time my life got way off track. I soon realized that summertime tended to bring out the best and the worst in people, places, and things, and living in the summertime was anything but easy for me!

"Summertime and the livin' is easy
Fish are jumpin', and the cotton is high.
Oh, your daddy's rich and your ma is good lookin'
So, hush, little baby, don't you cry,"
(Heyward, Gershwin & Gershwin, lyricists)

17

Turned On

'As the World Turns' made its television debut in April 1956, and it was on the air for fifty-four years. It was the second-longest-running television soap opera in America's history. Soap operas were the height of the day when I grew up. We called the television series, "the stories."

My grandparents' home was one place to watch the stories every day. My adoptive grandmother, Mama Penn, was devoted almost religiously to them. Mama Penn was a community babysitter, and she and my grandfather provided daycare for single mothers. Mama made sure all the children's needs were taken care of before the stories came on because nothing was to interfere with the television programs.

My favorite soap opera was "As the World Turns." I loved the opening scene with the overcast cloud on the revolving globe with soft background music. It seemed surreal. Really, my world was beginning to turn.

I came to believe I performed my "rite of passage" after I

finished junior high school. I wanted my autonomy and to live independently of my parents' rules. The summer following, I engaged with a controversial lifestyle that introduced me further to drugs, promiscuity, homosexuality, and criminality. I got turned on!

"Turned on" was a street term that meant somebody either bought or introduced someone else to drugs. The act of "turning someone on" served a myriad of purposes. Sometimes it was a tactic for drug dealers to involve other people in selling drugs, while other times, turning someone on allowed drug-crazed people to share their insanity with others. (Misery does love company!) "Turning on" someone was also used by sexual predators to lure people into sexual misconduct. Such was the case with my introduction to heroin when Kyle Murray "turned me on."

Kyle was about seven or eight years older than me, and he had a negative reputation in the community. He had had some escapades with the law, and he was a known school truant. Known around town as the only twenty-two-year-old person still in high school, his peers made fun of him. But he had a darker side.

There were rumors that Kyle, with a wooden instrument, sodomized a young male in the neighborhood, and he was arrested because of it. My parents were aware of his reputation, and they intensely disliked him. I was mostly oblivious to Kyle's character.

Kyle started to stalk me when I was about ten years old. I had no idea what he was doing, but I knew I should avoid him at all costs. He made further advances to me when I became a teenager. After I entered the homosexual lifestyle, Kyle solicited and coerced me to have sexual relationships with him, but I refused. He persisted, and he sought opportunities to be with me at the oddest places and times when no one else was around. Eventually, he gained access to me during my time of personal family loss.

My adoptive grandfather was named General Washington Penn, and we called him "Papa." He was highly revered in our family, church, and community, and he was my hero. My spiritual mentor, Papa, was a devoted follower of Jesus Christ, and he first brought me to church when I was four years old. After a brief bout with stomach cancer, Papa died on a Friday shortly after I started the ninth grade. The Friday Papa died; Kyle Murray showed up at my front door that night.

Mom and Dad had left home to make Papa's funeral arrangements, and somehow Kyle knew it. He knocked on my door as soon as my parents left. I was startled, and more so when he showed me, he had two or three bags of heroin with him. I thought it was like a bad dream!

I was afraid of drugs, although I had let my guard down by experimenting with marijuana a couple of months earlier. I figured smoking marijuana had been a brief phase, and I had no intention to continue using it. But that Friday night, everything changed when I was confronted by both my fears-heroin and Kyle Murray.

Kyle took the first nasal ingestion of heroin that evening, and he repeated the process two or three times before he passed the drugs to me. Clumsily, I lifted the heroin out of the glassine bag with a thin cocktail straw. Panicky on the inside, I nervously spilled some of the dope before I reached my nostrils with it. I snorted the heroin, and then I tasted something bitter. Soon, there was a postnasal drip as secretions of the heroin slid through my nasal passages and into my esophagus. I felt a little numb and wondered if I was high? At first, it made no sense to me, then, about fifteen minutes later, I sensed a slight unfamiliar euphoria. As I tried to familiarize myself with the obscure feeling, suddenly, I heard a door key. My parents had returned home. I was petrified!

"Be sober-minded; be watchful. Your adversary the devil prowls around like a roaring lion, seeking someone to devour. Resist him, firm in your faith, knowing that the same kinds of suffering are being experienced by your brotherhood throughout the world"
(1 Peter 5:8-9).

18

Caught!

My heart couldn't beat faster, and I wanted to jump out of our sixth floor living room window. I gave my full attention to the sound of the door key as I waited every second for the door to swing open. I prayed it was not real, but the key kept turning. I thought I was going to die.

Ma unlocked the door, and she was the first one to walk inside the apartment. I wanted to stand up and scream, "Wait, don't come in yet. First, let me fix the mess I'm in. It's my fault, and I can make it right!" But it was too late. There was no way to cover up the mess. I was caught!

Kyle Murray, with his street meticulousness, hid the heroin from Ma's view. I sat motionless on our plastic-covered blue sofa as my mother saw her worst nightmare before her eyes, Kyle Murray sitting in our apartment. I couldn't move off the couch. Ma was furious. After being speechless for a moment, she demanded Kyle to leave our house immediately. She threatened him and ordered him never to return. Ma hardly ever used profanity, but she may have spoken out of her character that night. I was in shock!

My mother was not only furious, but she was also hurt. I had disappointed her and my father beyond any degree. Guilty, I sat motionlessly on the sofa, and I couldn't say anything as Ma fumed. It was horrible. Dad agreed with her every rebuke. My parents were loving, but I knew I was in deep trouble. I kept wishing it had been a bad dream.

The rest of the night became a blur. I didn't remember much about the ordeal or what my parents said. All I could remember was that Papa, my hero, and spiritual mentor, had also died that day! I could see Papa's bedroom window from our apartment, and I looked towards his window before I turned off my bedroom light. Suddenly I realized something else died. My dreams, hopes, and aspirations were terminated in thirty unforgettable regrettable minutes and I was caught!

"Even youths shall faint and be weary, and young men shall fall exhausted; but they who wait for the LORD shall renew their strength; they shall mount up with wings like eagles; they shall run and not be weary; they shall walk and not faint"
(Isaiah 40:30–31).

19

Trapped

The Vietnam War heightened during my teenage years, and I worried about the US military draft. The mandatory selection ended as the Vietnam War concluded in April 1975. I felt fortunate that I hadn't been selected by the army. I volunteered for another combat instead.

Simultaneous to my debut with heroin, I enlisted in the "hippie" subculture, which I was happy to be a part of it. I wanted to be on the front-line of the new movement, and my life changed as I imbibed the culture and discarded authority, morality, and Christianity. I forfeited dignity and traditional values to gain the badges of the counterrevolution.

I progressed quickly from ingesting heroin nasally to injecting it under my skin (skin-popping it was called). That phase lasted for about two weeks. Soon after, I no longer experienced the euphoria I had started to idolize. Cold chills, sweats, and lethargy were more frequent when I didn't do drugs.

I needed to use more heroin to achieve the desired and needed effects, or I could "mainline" (inject the dope in my veins) for potent results. The choice was simple. I was a teenaged addict in a poor, mostly black southside neighborhood, and I didn't have money to buy drugs to start with. The product of a misguided and "lost" culture; I started to mainline, and I was trapped.

A news reporter wrote in a 1970 New York Times article, *Kids and Heroin: The Adolescent Epidemic,* that heroin had been made available to teenagers in the ghettos for twenty years. Claude Brown documented the atrocity in his book, *Man Child in the Promised Land,* as early as 1950. The reporter said that heroin was an indescribable nightmare. "It is infamous as the hardest of drugs, the notorious nepenthe of the most hopeless narcotics addicts, the toughest of monkeys for anyone to get off his back."

I had promised myself I'd never use drugs, and I imagined a heroin addict was the worse any person could be. Then, I became that person. Consumed by a false definition of life, I assumed a charade of parties, alcohol, heroin, and free sex was the ideal. I sought people, places, and things that helped make my interpretation a reality. But my understanding was a false narrative, and I got it wrong. Life was more precious and valuable than I knew or believed. I needed to know the truth to be free.

"The thief comes only to steal and kill and destroy. I came that they may have life and have it more abundantly"
(John 10:10).

20

Bad to Worse

I chose to do what I wanted to do, rather than obey what I knew was right. Sin has had its roots in selfishness since the Fall of humanity resulting from Adam and Eve's disobedience to God's command (Genesis 3:1-19). I heard a preacher say that sin takes a person farther than they want to go; keeps them longer than he or she wants to stay; and makes the person pay more than they want to pay! I didn't anticipate the consequences of my decisions to sin, but the ramifications caused me many regrets. Then, things got worse.

It was a Thursday afternoon when my school guidance counselor called me out of my 7th-period class. Miss Berger, the counselor, told me I had a telephone call when I arrived at her office. I was surprised! I had never received a phone call at school. Miss Berger gave me the phone. "Nana" was on the other end of the phone.

Hi Nana," I said with usual politeness as I clutched the phone. She replied, "*Hi, Donnie.*" Nana sounded calm with her usual strength and firm Christian character. I tried to quickly think about what might be wrong. Nana said, "*Donnie, there's been an accident, and I don't want you to worry, but Lucille had an accident."* I froze for a few minutes, while Nana paused.

Recently, Nana (Mrs. Adelaide Dawson) had become close to our family (the Johnsons) as she struggled to raise three of her grandchildren. By God's providence, she asked Mama Lucille to rear her youngest grandson, Marcel. Lucille agreed, and Marcel was four years old when he came to live with us. I was happy to have him as a baby brother. I was grateful that Nana and her family had become a part of ours.

Nana went on to explain to me that my adoptive mother had fallen down a steep flight of concrete steps in one of our local department stores that afternoon. Oh no, I thought, will Ma make it? How bad is she hurt? Immediately, I thought the worse. Then, Nana added, *"Lucille is okay, but she's in the hospital. You get over there as soon as you can. OK?"* I said, *"Yes, Nana."* I was terrified as I hung up the phone.

Ma was a sickly woman for most of my life. During my formative years, she had been a weekend alcoholic, but she stopped drinking. She credited me for that, and she told me she stopped drinking so she could raise me appropriately. Ma was frequently ill, even after she stopped drinking, and I worried about her. I was obsessed with fear and the idea she would die before I reached adulthood.

Every year, my tension exacerbated when Ma went into the hospital for treatment of her primary chronic disease, diverticulitis, an inflammatory illness, especially in the colon. After Nana's phone call to me in school, I wondered if this was the time that Ma would leave, abandon me. I left the school guidance office, and I rushed to the hospital.

21

Life Changed

Mount Victory Hospital was only two miles from the high school, but it seemed like the public bus took an eternity to get me to the medical center. Ma was still in the Emergency Room when I arrived. The hospital staff brought me immediately to her bedside.

I saw an array of bloody sheets and towels on the hospital stretcher before I went inside my mother's curtain closed cubicle. From the sheets and towels on the cot, it appeared every bone in Ma's body was broken. She was wrapped in bloody hospital linen from her waist down. I was in shock as I stood and looked at her on the stretcher. I was speechless.

Ma's smile was the only thing that kept me from falling apart. She smiled at me as I walked inside her cubicle, despite the incredible pain she experienced. Somehow, her smile gave me the courage to believe she would survive the tragic accident. Ma was an incredible woman.

A devoted wife, mother, and grandmother, her smile reflected love, wisdom, and inner strength. She was the matriarch and pillar of our family, and she had a special love for people. Employed as a nurse's aide for special needs children, Ma mentored and counseled countless women and their families. She was dearly beloved, and I did not want to lose her.

I dreaded my fears as Ma laid almost totally incapacitated in the Emergency Room. *Would she live through this?* "*Would she pull through,*" I asked myself repeatedly. Then, I prayed. "*Donnie, Mommy's going to be alright,*" I heard my mother say. I sighed in relief, but I had a hard time overcoming the sight of her paralyzed body drenched with the hospital linens. Ma's life would not be the same.

My mother was in the hospital for six months, and she underwent numerous surgeries to break and reset many of her bones. She had to learn to walk again, and she used a walker and a cane for the remainder of her life. She never completely recovered from the accident, but her health resumed some normalcy. However, I, myself, went from bad to worse. Life changed!

> "*Many are the afflictions of the righteous, but the LORD delivers him out of them all*"
> (Psalm 34:19).

22

"Home Alone"

"Who then is the faithful and wise manager, whom his master will set over his household, to give them their portion of food at the proper time? Blessed is that servant whom his master will find so doing when he comes"
(Luke 12:42-43).

My mother's accident resulted in changes for her and our family. It had an emotional impact on all of us. I tried to adjust to our "new normal," but my mother's hospitalization and absence from the home fortified my drug dependency and truancy. Often, I was home alone.

Dad was present in the house during the day, but he worked at night as a security guard. His work shift was from 10:00 pm to 6:00 am, and I was home alone during those times. It was not a good arrangement. Sixteen years old and a heroin addict, I took advantage of the situation. I converted our apartment into a night-time "shooting gallery" for other heroin users. The word got out on the street.

Someone always needed a place to do drugs, and addicts rang my doorbell as soon as Dad left for work. People were in and out of the apartment all night long. Sometimes, I'd get two or three hours of sleep before I went to school. Hungover, I managed to stay in school for three or four hours at most. Then off to see Ma in the hospital where I pretended my life was okay. But everything wasn't okay.

I had been a Regents and college-bound student, but that changed. My heroin addiction and all-night house parties took their toll. My grades dropped dramatically, and my drug dependency increased. Ma knew something was wrong, and she started to confront me while she was still in the hospital. But I lied and denied I had any problems. I convinced myself that I could still manage my life.

Later, my parents were severely disappointed when they realized I was in trouble. What had they done wrong? Had they not been good parents? They probably wondered if adopting me was a mistake. But the failure was not in them; It was in me. I was home alone, and I couldn't handle it.

"Take care, brothers, lest there be in any of you an evil, unbelieving heart, leading you to fall away from the living God. But exhort one another every day, as long as it is called 'today,' that none of you may be hardened by the deceitfulness of sin" (Hebrews 3:12–13).

23

No place to hide!

Mount Victory High School was a drug haven by early 1970, and a variety of drugs was sold on the school campus. Most of the student-drug dealers sold narcotics, while others pushed marijuana and psychedelic drugs. The high school was a maze of dealings, dropouts, and student-addicts who regularly overdosed. It was an insane social scene!

The narcotics police surveilled our high school regularly, and school officials mandated drug testing for suspected users. I was surprised to hear that my name was on the drug testing list. I was one of the most conspicuous drug users in the school, but I denied it. I cut classes and dodged the school nurse to avoid drug testing, but there was an entity I couldn't escape. It was the police!

I started to feel uneasiness at home and in school. My mother added to my anxiety when she told me she had a dream about me. Ma never told me about her dream, but I knew it was bad since she concealed it from me. Probably she hoped it wouldn't come true. But there was no place to hide. I had a looming sense that "something" was going to happen.

Massive gray clouds hung over Mount Victory's southside as I prepared for high school that Wednesday morning in October '71. The weather looked threatening, and I was anxious because there were rumors the narcotics detectives had been in the school the previous week to arrest me. The atmosphere was tense when I arrived at school. None of the usual students were in the hallways, and the school monitors weren't around. The teachers hadn't gathered for their morning chats and faculty updates, and everything was eerie!

My fear went through the roof when the school secretary came to my first-period class. Silently, she passed a slip of paper to my homeroom teacher. My teacher walked over to me immediately, and he gave me the sheet of paper. He instructed me to report to Division F, my guidance counselor's office. I almost froze.

It was a four or five-minute walk to the guidance office. I walked into the counselor's office, and then my reality and fears collided. The narcotics detectives were there, and they had come to arrest me. I had no place to hide!

The cops greeted me with a friendly smile and acted as if they were to become my new best friends. "This can't be real," I thought. I didn't know what to expect next. The detectives had a search warrant, so they brought me to my home to search the apartment. Someone told them I was in possession of narcotic implements (a needle and syringe). My possession was illegal, and the police used the narcotic instruments to charge me and place me under arrest.

The police escorted me out of their car, and we went upstairs to my apartment. I brought them into my bedroom, where I retrieved the drug paraphernalia, and I gave it to the officers. Suddenly one of the police reached for both my wrists. Before I knew anything, I heard a loud click. The police had handcuffed me, and I couldn't move my wrists or hands. I couldn't believe it was happening. There was no place to hide!

"Hear my cry, O God, listen to my prayer; from the end of the earth I call to you when my heart is faint, lead me to the rock that is higher than I"
(Psalm 61:1-2).

24

Broke, Busted, and Disgusted!

"A wise son makes a glad father, but a foolish son is a sorrow to his mother"
(Proverbs 10:1).

Ma cried and begged the police not to bring me to jail. The detectives tried to reassure her and said that they were taking me to get help for my addiction. They lied. The police took me from the police car, criminally processed me in the local police department, and then, I was locked up in the city jail. Later, they transported me to the county jail about fifteen miles away. My bond for release was $1500, and I figured I'd be in jail for a while. My parents didn't have the money or any other means of collateral to post my bail. I awaited my next day in court.

Several court appearances later, my bail was reduced to $500 cash. Amazingly, by that time, my mother had incurred a monetary settlement from her accident, and my parents paid the cash bond. I was thankful. But I couldn't ignore my parents' anguish, nor that I had regressed to a jailbird.

The court case dragged on and on, during which I incurred another arrest. Coerced by DaShaun once again, the two of us committed a crime that was far more serious than my first offense. I faced a prison sentence of seven to twenty-five years, as a result.

I was terrified of spending *years* in prison with high school graduation just months away. I asked the LORD to save me out of the situation. I was desperate, and the first thing, the only thing I knew to do was *pray*! Both arrests gave me opportunities to put my faith in action. I was grateful for my church upbringing, and I valued my grandfather's spiritual mentorship more than ever! I prayed like I had not done before. God answered my prayers, and his grace brought me this far!

"Now the law came in to increase the trespass, but where sin increased, grace abounded all the more, so that as sin reigned in death, grace also might reign through righteousness leading to eternal life through Jesus Christ our Lord,"
(Romans 5:20–21).

25

Let God Arise!

"But when he came to himself, he said, how many of my father's hired servants have more than enough bread, but I perish here with hunger! I will arise and go to my father, and I will say to him, "Father, I have sinned against heaven and before you" (Luke 15:17-18).

I leaned heavily on my faith after I became involved with the law. My theology was not profoundly developed, but I had faith in God's goodness and mercy. I remembered the manifestations of God's presence when I was a child.

The Holy Spirit's presence was often tangible in our small black church. People lifted their hands and praised God as they were touched by the Spirit. Others would cry and "shout" as they were overwhelmed by the Holy Ghost. Also, I witnessed God's provision and care during those challenging times in the economy and society. God always provided! I knew he helped people in trouble.

I believed God would intervene in my situation if I committed to not return to jail. I sincerely did not want to spend my life in prison. My faith prompted me to write a letter to the judge and plead for the court's mercy.

I sat at the kitchen table across from the living room where I first ingested heroin with Kyle Murray. My faith in God increased as I thought about the words for the letter. As I typed each word one key at a time on my dad's manual typewriter, I felt a love for the Lord. I regretted my situation. I said in the letter:

> *Dear Judge Paulin:*
>
> *I am sorry for the crime I committed. I was forced into it by my friend. I admit I was wrong, and I am sorry. I ask you to give me another chance to finish high school. I have been an Honor Roll student, and I plan to go to college. I want to become a fashion designer, a lawyer, or a teacher. I will never return to your court again. I pray you can find it in your heart to give me another chance. Thank you for your leniency and the court's mercy.*

I was surprised during my subsequent court appearance that Judge Paulin advised the court he received and read my letter. Before he granted my request, the judge reminded me of the commitments I made. He sentenced me to Shock Probation, a sentence that included thirty days in the county jail and five years on probation. I was grateful I wouldn't spend seven or more years in prison, but I was terrified in another way.

I avowed to the judge and court that I'd stay out of trouble, but I wondered if I was truly willing to do so. The only way I'd succeed was to forfeit my self-will and stop the rebellious living and idolatry. More importantly, I needed to trust God with my life and future.

> *"Trust in the LORD with all your heart, and do not lean on your own understanding. In all your ways acknowledge him, and he will make straight your paths"*
> *(Proverbs 3:5–6).*

26

Unlearned!

Jails and prisons have perpetuated degradation in human beings for centuries. Early penal establishments with intimidating structures and pestilent environments made prisoners pay with institutionalization and fear and remorse. I never forgot my experience as a young prisoner in the county correctional facility. The experience made me fear the prospect of becoming a career criminal.

I was ashamed, guilty, and vulnerable to others. The effects of incarceration helped me keep my vow to never return to jail. And with God's grace and his intervention, I never did. Getting out of jail was a *real* breath of fresh air for me, but unfortunately, I had not learned my lesson.

Humiliated as I was by the jail experience, it didn't deter me from using drugs and alcohol. I was physically and psychologically addicted to drugs, and I persisted in other risky and harmful behaviors as well. It was only by God's grace I was not re-arrested. I hoped high school graduation would come soon so I could go out of state to attend college. I thought going away would help me change. But when I moved to Washington, D.C. to attend college, I didn't overcome my problems, they became worse!

> *"Because you have ignored all my counsel and would have none of my reproof, I also will laugh at your calamity; I will mock when terror strikes you"*
> *(Proverbs 1:25-27).*

27

Stop the World I want to get off!

Recently I heard a preacher in Dallas, Texas, tell a story about a young girl who attended the New York World's Fair in the 1960s. The girl's father bought several tickets for his daughter to ride some of the attractions. The child became fascinated with the roller coaster, and repeatedly, she used another coupon and then another to ride on the roller coaster. Finally, as the fair started to close, the young girl realized she had experienced only one ride. Suddenly, she asked her father to take her to the other amusements. However, she had run out of tickets. Anxiously, she asked her father to purchase more tickets so she could get on the other rides. But unfortunately, as the fair closed, no more tickets could be bought. It was mostly a wasted day for the little girl at the World's Fair, one might say!

America was shocked to learn the tragic news that Diane Linkletter, high on LSD, jumped out of the sixth-floor window in her West Hollywood, California apartment, and she committed suicide. Diane's father, Art Linkletter, was America's affable, fatherly, and beloved radio and TV personality. He became a catalyst for America's war on drugs after his daughter's death. The nation realized the countercultural revolution had crossed social barriers and penetrated political guard rails. Parents, elders, and religious leaders in local communities prayed and braced themselves with "supernatural steel" as they awaited news of the next person to die from a heroin overdose or commit suicide.

Miraculously, I finished high school after my escapades with the law. Mount Victory High School wanted nothing more than to get "the problem kids" off the campus. I barely graduated, but nonetheless, my parents were ecstatic when I walked across the stage to receive my diploma. They knew I had come that far by God's grace!

I moved to Washington, D.C., to attend Strayer College, and I became more involved in drugs. I met some affluent kids who went to Georgetown University, and they introduced me to psychedelic drugs and LSD. Flashbacks and "bad trips" became my new normal! I knew I couldn't survive there for long, so I returned to New York after being in D.C. for one and a half years. I resumed my habit with heroin.

It was the early summer of 1972, just before our family moved out of the housing projects and purchased a home. A new batch of heroin hit the Mount Victory city streets, and it caught on like wildfire. Little did I know that people were overdosing from the potent heroin all over Southern New York. Naively, I bought a bag of heroin and went into my bedroom to "shoot it up."

I felt confident I knew just the right amount to use to get high, and at the same time, avoid an overdose. Slowly, I injected the heroin, but before I finished pumping it into my vein, I fell into a deep non-euphoric sleep. I had overdosed. It would be minutes until the heroin eclipsed my life, but God's grace was amazing.

Rock Morris, a friend, knocked on my front door while I overdosed in my bedroom. My mother knew nothing of the situation, but she let Rock in and told him I was in my room. Shocked by what he saw, Rock started to slap me in my face with his bare hands and forcefully tried to wake me up. I awoke briefly but drifted back and forth into death's valley. Quickly with an ability like "a street healer," Rock took the needle out of my arm and filled the syringe with table salt and water. Then, he shot the solution into my veins. Abruptly, the death antidote woke me up from the stupor. I was so close to termination that my body was numb, and it felt like dead weight. By God's grace, I awoke from the overdose, and God used Rock Morris to save me.

I wasted a lot of years by my persistent roller coaster rides with sin and lawless ideations. I was on a hopeless merry-go-round, and the longer I rode it, the more my life was disoriented. Inside, I pleaded for the world to stop, so I could get off! It was a struggle to get off the roller-coaster, but "struggle" is a prerequisite to surrender."[21] Eventually, I surrendered my life to Jesus Christ, and I overcame my destructive lifestyle.

"And they have conquered him by the blood of the Lamb and by the word of their testimony, for they loved not their lives even unto death" (Revelation 12:11).

28

🌿

Valley of the Dolls!

Deceived by a false sense of invincibility, I was shocked I overdosed on heroin, and I was even more surprised I survived the catastrophe. God's grace was amazing in my life, yet I persisted in my addictions. I progressed to abuse amphetamines also known as "speed" and diet pills.

Amphetamines, classified as stimulant drugs, cause messages between the brain and the body to accelerate. It stimulates the brain to release dopamine, a chemical that affects mood, thinking, and movement. Dopamine, the body's "feel-good" chemical, makes the user more alert and physically active. Regularly, people used "speed" to enhance their athletic performance, stay awake on their job, or even to study for an exam.[22] Methamphetamine, a type of amphetamine, has gained widespread street use today.

I had not heard of amphetamines early in my addiction. "Speed" was not the drug of choice for my friends and me in our southside communities. Surprisingly, the drug (commonly called diet pills) became available in my neighborhood in the early 1980s.

I was introduced to "diet pills" by one of my close female friends. My friend seemed unaffected by the "speed" after an hour or so, but almost immediately, I experienced a chemical euphoria I had not known. The drug made me feel light-headed, energetic, brave, and very confident. I was addicted to it almost instantly, and not long after, I did anything to acquire the diet pills.

I fabricated a weight problem to get doctors to write me prescriptions, and I bribed my overweight girlfriends to sell me their medicines. I was obsessed with the "speed" and I liked it, but I did not know the real dangers. Amphetamines have been known to cause psychosis.

In 1966, Jacqueline Susann published the novel, *Valley of the Dolls*, and I read the book from cover to cover. The bestselling book was turned into a movie in 1967. The title song and Dionne Warwick's voice echoed the cultural revolution's essence.

Valley of the Dolls was about middle-class people who succumbed to amphetamine addiction and the prescription drug crisis in the 1960s and '70s. Cast in the turbulent, counter-cultural societies of New York City and Hollywood, the story involved three young white middle-class women with different personalities and backgrounds. The trio converged in New York City and became friends fast. Commonly, each woman shared their ambition and proclivity to fall in love with the wrong men. Jacqueline Susann wrote about her characters' abuse of alcohol, amphetamines, and barbiturates as the trio's lives became more strained and complicated.

Neely O'Hara was my favorite character in the film. Portrayed by Patty Duke, an Oscar award winner in 1963, Neely O'Hara was a bright, talented, and upcoming Broadway singer. Helen

Lawson (Anita Hayward) despised Neely because of her talent, and she wanted Neely fired from their Broadway play. But as fate would have it, Neely became an overnight success through another acting opportunity.

Unfortunately, her victory made her vain and self-confident. Neely's career was shattered by her erratic behavior, abuse of amphetamines and barbiturates, and infidelity. She was the first to be committed to a psychiatric hospital for rehabilitation. Later in the film and by the movie's end, all the characters were admitted to the mental hospital as victims of addiction, mental breakdowns, unfulfilled dreams, and heartbreak.

The story was etched my mind! I didn't know the theatrical depiction would become my reality, and I would experience a "valley of the dolls," a deep, dark place of helplessness and no self-control. But thanks be to God. He brought me this far by his grace!

"Rejoice, O young man, in your youth, and let your heart cheer you..Walk in the ways of your heart and the sight of your eyes. But know that for all these things God will bring you in judgment..for youth and the dawn of life are vanity" (Ecclesiastes 11:9–10).

29

⚜

Bugged Out!

Rumors went around town that I had lost my mind. People whispered to each other when they saw me in the neighborhood, and familiar friends briefly said "hello" and kept walking. Others did not know what to say, so they said nothing. Some people wondered what was wrong with me while others affirmed I "bugged out." The rumors were correct. I had succumbed to psychosis, quite like the characters in *Valley of the Dolls*.

Psychosis, a significant mental disorder, has been known to impair personality to the point of disorganization. It causes a person to lose contact with external reality.[23] I didn't see it coming, but I began suffering from severe paranoia. At first, I could function somewhat normally while I worked and lived in the community, but my mental state deteriorated. I was constantly plagued by auditory hallucinations and delusions.

I heard "voices," no one else heard, and I responded abruptly. I believed someone wiretapped my apartment, and people and groups were conspiring against me. Also, I imagined myself caught in a love triangle. Deluded further, I was convinced there was a conspiracy to kidnap my biological mother. The deception urged me to embark on a mission to "save her."

In several psychotic attempts, I hurled myself in front of moving cars to rescue my mother from "*her kidnappers.*" More times than I remember, I walked to the roof of my twenty-one-story apartment building, to calculate how to get to the adjacent building to save her. Eventually, I was arrested in the hospital's maternity ward, where I thought my mother's enemies held her hostage. But my mother did not need to be saved, I did. Satan had a plan to destroy my life, but God saved me! I came this far by his grace!

> *"I waited patiently for the LORD; he inclined to me and heard my cry, He drew me up from the pit of destruction, out of the miry bog, and set my feet upon a rock, making my steps secure. He put a new song in my mouth, a song of praise to our God"* (Psalm 40:1–3).

30

Moving Up, then Out!

I had been in my thirties when I moved into the Westchester Plaza apartments. The apartments were constructed in the early 1970s as the result of urban renewal efforts. The development was one of the few posh buildings in town. Living in the Plaza was bittersweet for me because I reached my ultimate addiction and alcoholism while I lived there. I experienced alcohol blackouts soon after I moved in.

Frequently, after an alcohol and prescription drug binge, I didn't wake up until days later without realizing what day it was. My psychosis worsened, and I was more unstable. Eventually, I was court marshaled and evicted from The Plaza for non-payment of rent. It was a hard pill to swallow while I was hospitalized in a psychiatric institution.

One psychiatric hospitalization led to another. At thirty-four years old, drug dependent, possibly borderline schizophrenic, homeless, unsaved, I felt hopeless. I began believing my life and situation would not change, and I wouldn't get better. I was disappointed with myself, and I was tired of letting down my family and other people who cared about me. My vision for life and a future were dim. I started sleeping in the stairwell in a tenement building as I tried to avoid people and reality. I did not want to face my circumstances, and I thought the Lord might *graciously* allow me to die in my sorrow and shame.

I tried to deny that God had created me for more than I experienced, but the Holy Spirit never affirmed my self-doubt. I couldn't discredit God's ability, and that he could transform (change) me if I gave him the opportunity. I thought about becoming a true Christian, and I knew it was a better life than mine. I was becoming desperate for Jesus!

> "If I ascend to heaven, you are there! If I make my bed in Sheol, you are there. If I take the wings of the morning and dwell in the uttermost parts of the sea, even there your hand shall lead me, and your right hand shall hold me"
> (Psalm 139:8–10).

31

Redeemed!

I was still trying to piece together my identity, overcome deep-seated rejection, and find acceptance when I started listening to a religious TV broadcast from Dallas, Texas. The program held my attention, and I looked forward to Sundays when the program aired. I was not attending church, but the religious program reminded me of my youth. Part of me longed for the joy I had as "a child of God."

My thinking started to change as I became sick and tired of the way I lived. More and more, I thought about "getting saved." My family and religious leaders had told me numerous times that I *had* to be born again. Biblically, they explained that no one enters heaven without being born again. Several aspects of my life conflicted with my religious upbringing, but almost in an instant, I decided to ask more about "being born again." I wrote a letter to the TV evangelist.

After listening to the TV preacher a few times, I gained the confidence to write and reveal my sins to him. I had never confessed my sins to anyone, but I knew confessing (and letting go) them was a prerequisite for being born again. After all, the TV preacher didn't know me, and he wouldn't reject me because of my sins. I didn't know if the preacher would read my letter or what would happen after he did. But one day, I received a response from him. I was surprised! The evangelist said something like this:

"Donald, God has heard your cry. Jesus has made you free. Whoever the Son makes free, they are free indeed. If you confess with your mouth, the Lord Jesus, and believe in your heart that God has raised him from the dead, you will be saved (Romans 10:10). Do you believe it? Will you confess Jesus today?" he asked.

I was encouraged by his letter, and immediately I followed his instructions. It was easy for me to confess Jesus Christ as Savior because I grew up believing and learning about Christ. Of course, I believed, and I knew Jesus was "the way, the truth, and the life."

I wrote the evangelist again and told him I had accepted Jesus as my Lord and Savior. To my surprise, he wrote me once more and congratulated me on becoming a Christian. I praised God. I was redeemed!

"For godly grief produces a repentance that leads to salvation without regret, whereas worldly grief produces death"
(2 Corinthians 7:10).

32

🌿

The Defining Moment!

I did well for some time after I accepted Christ. I gained courage and wisdom to avoid people, places, and things that provoked me to substance abuse. However, sexual promiscuity and immorality lurked in the tethered places in my life, and I hadn't totally surrendered.

I continued to rely on pornography and prescription meds for self-gratification. After a while, without discipleship and consistent church attendance, I stopped trying to be an overcomer. I relapsed. The relapse led me into deeper and more profound abuse, and my situation was much worse (seven times) than before I had accepted Christ. I knew the problem was not with God or his plan of salvation; it was my lack of true repentance, turning away from sin and towards God.

I was back in the psychiatric hospital for the third time in 1988. Doctors suspected I had developed schizophrenia as the result of prolonged drug abuse. They recommended I take psychotropic medications for the rest of my life, and possibly live full-time in a residential facility. That was a defining moment for me.

The familiar psychiatric social worker greeted me when I arrived in the hospital, and she waived the admission intake. Dressed professionally in a form-fitted beige skirt and crisp looking white blouse, I noticed the young woman's demeanor was different. The social worker had a stern look on her face. *"Mr. Johnson,* she said, *"you have to get better."* I stood still for a moment at her blatant statement, and I knew she was telling the truth. My immediate impulse was to run and hide, but instead, I processed her words.

I thought, "Me? Do you mean *I* must get better?" I wanted to ask. I had depended on psychiatry, drugs, and promiscuity for a long time. But the social worker afforded me a new challenge, an opportunity to take responsibility for my healing.

For the first time in twenty-one years, I realized I had a part to play in overcoming the addictions, psychosis, domestic abuse, homelessness, and everything that devastated me. It was overwhelming, but I had a little hope that something revolutionary might happen if I acquiesced. It was my time to ask God for forgiveness and for him to be genuinely involved in my life.

That wintry afternoon in New York, I sat on the bedside in the mentally ill chemically addicted unit, and I recited some words from Psalm 23. I said, *"The Lord is my shepherd; I shall not want. He makes me lie down in green pastures. He leads me beside still waters. He restoreth my soul..."* At that instance, I surrendered everything to Jesus. It was a Kairos moment,

"I will lift up my eyes to the hills. From where does my help come? My help comes from the Lord, who made heaven and earth" (Psalm 121:1-2).

33

Throw out the Lifeline!

I had to confront homelessness upon my release from the mental hospital. I had never been without a home, and I wasn't prepared to live in a homeless shelter. I considered feigning some additional psychosis to stay longer in the hospital, but I mustered the courage to face reality.

I accepted I'd live in a shelter since I had reached out to family, but most were reluctant or not in a position to house me. But one family member, Betty Johnson Bethany, had a lot of faith in God, and a willingness to help me. She was a younger aunt of mine on the Johnsons' side.

Betty and I were almost the same age, and we grew up together. At one point, she moved back to Mississippi, where she attended school until her original birth records were secured. She returned to New York while we were in high school.

Betty became a committed Christian who practiced "what she preached," and she was very hospitable. She had rescued me from near homelessness on another occasion, and when she discovered

I had been sleeping in a stairwell, she was ready to intervene again. I was grateful to Betty, and because of her, I didn't live in a shelter for more than a day or two.

It was during the Christmas season, a couple of days before the New Year when I was released from the hospital and went to Betty's home. Soon, "Watch Night Service" would be held in almost every church in town. "Watch Night Service" marked the end of the year, and people gathered to pray for the new one. I was certain I'd be in church as 1988 ended. I had made an appointment with God. I planned to meet with him on "Watch Night" at the altar. Jesus threw out "The Lifeline!"

"Blessed are the pure in heart, for they shall see God"
(Matthew 5:8).

34

New Year, New Rules!

"You ascended on high, leading a host of captives in your train and receiving gifts among men, even among the rebellious, that the LORD God may dwell there"
(Psalm 68:18).

The *"Watch Night service"* tradition has been traced back to the early 18th century. Reportedly, Moravian churchgoers made a vigil on December 31st, and they reflected on the past and prayed for the coming year. Congregants praised God for what he had done, and they asked him to grant his blessings in the New Year. The vigil culminated at midnight.[24]

The Watch Night tradition extended to other mainline Protestant denominations. John Wesley, a leader of a revival movement within the Anglican church, adopted the observance for his Methodist followers. Regularly, the Methodists held "watch night" vigils each month in correspondence with the full moons.[25] In 1862, the traditional church service gained new significance.

African slaves prayed, sang hymns, and thanked God in private homes and churches in the confederate states on December 31st. The slaves' most important prayer was for freedom, however. They prayed that the Emancipation Proclamation would take full effect on January 1st.[26] The "Watch Night" Gathering was not in vain, and God answered the slaves' prayers.

On January 1, 1863, President Abraham Lincoln signed the Emancipation Proclamation changing the federal legal status of more than 3.5 million African slaves. It was a political victory for the denouncement of slavery and injustice. The executive order reflected God's faithfulness and his redemptive history.

God was faithful in delivering the Israelites' out of Egyptian bondage and slavery by "the hand of Moses." Through sovereign political maneuvering, he enabled the Jews to return to Jerusalem from their Babylonian captivity. Then, God sent Jesus Christ to die and procure eternal emancipation for all people who accept him as Lord and Savior. I received my personal emancipation in 1989.

Upon my release from the psychiatric hospital, I decided 1989 would be different. *New Year, New Rules* was my adoptive mother's philosophy. Before each new year, she reiterated the statement, which meant she and my father would not tolerate the craziness and rebellion I exhibited the past year. I needed to adjust because with the new year came new rules also. Finally, I was ready!

I arrived early at the church on the evening of December 31st. I made my way to the front of the worship center, and I sat close to the altar. I knew the pastors would have an altar call and invite people to pray just before the New Year dawned. After the songs, adulations, and sermons, it was time to pray!

Bravely, I kneeled at the altar in the front of the church, and I prayed. I thanked God for his goodness and for rescuing me from death and destruction. I asked him to fill me with the Holy Spirit as I surrendered everything to him. I had decided to follow Jesus for the rest of my life, and I kept thanking him for bringing me so far by grace!

"Bless the LORD, O my soul, and forget not all his benefits, who forgives all your iniquity, who heals all your diseases"
(Psalm 103:2–3).

35

🌿

Changed by the Holy Spirit

I surrendered my life to the Lord in December 1988, but before then, I had had "a Pentecostal experience" about two years earlier. I had encountered the Holy Spirit in a genuine and personal way as God's presence filled me in a prayer service. I was aware something supernatural had happened to me, but I didn't fully understand. Without discipleship, I did not know about the empowering and transforming work of the Holy Spirit to change lives. Later after I totally surrendered, I realized the significance of discipleship, consistent church attendance, and the various spiritual disciplines (prayer, fasting, Bible reading, meditation, and memorization). A Christian is a disciple (follower) of Jesus Christ.

Although the actual word "discipleship" is not in the Bible, "People need to become Christians and be taught how to think and feel and act as Christian. That is, a disciple, a follower of Jesus, one who embraces him as Lord and Savior and Treasure."[27] I learned how to become an authentic Christian in community with other believers, as I attended church several times a week. I loved hearing the believers' testimonies, and they helped me better appreciate *my new life in Christ*. I marveled that God had brought all of us a very long way by his grace! God restored my love for him and the church, and my desire to worship him deepened daily.

One day while I was praying and thanking God for his amazing grace, I remembered that Wednesday night in Bible class when Deacon Jones said to me, *"You're gonna be a preacher."* I was stunned for a minute as I recalled his statement. Could Deacon Jones have been right? Was I going to be a preacher? I quickly tried to dismiss the twenty-five years old prophecy, and I hoped my love and gratitude for God's grace *wouldn't* make me a preacher! Soon, I found out.

"But I received mercy for this reason, that in me, as the foremost, Jesus Christ might display his perfect patience as an example to those who were to believe in him for eternal life"
(1 Timothy 1:16).

36

Glad to be in His service!

*"For a day in your courts is better than a thousand
elsewhere. I would rather be a doorkeeper in the house
of my God than to dwell in the tents of wickedness"
(Psalm 84:10).*

I loved listening to the choirs in the Sunday church services, and
the Gospel Chorus was my favorite. The Gospel Chorus sang
all the hit gospel songs, and the members' voices harmonized
perfectly. I admired the choir enough to ask to join. Gary Davis,
the choir's president, welcomed me.

Shortly after I joined the choir, Gary relocated to upstate New
York. Before he moved, he asked me to succeed him as the choir's
president. I thought he was joking. "Gary," I said, "I just became
a member of the church. How…?" Quickly he replied, "That's ok!
The Lord has blessed you, and you can do it. I feel like God wants
you to be the next president of the Gospel Chorus." I couldn't
believe it.

I felt inadequate to be a church leader in any capacity. However, I was sure about my love for the Lord, and I was willing to do anything to express my gratitude. I accepted Gary's appointment, and the responsibility of "choir president" was my first church leadership role.

I dedicated myself to the leadership of the choir, and I developed good relationships with the choir members and others in the local congregation. My senior pastor became aware of my spiritual gifts. Then, a sudden turn of events occurred.

One day the senior pastor called me at home. "Brother Johnson," he said in his deep baritone voice, "I want you to start wearing a tie. You are a theologian now!" For a moment, I was in awe that the senior pastor called me, and I had to catch my breath. I was just a new member of the church. Then I realized what the pastor had said, "*I want you to start wearing a tie.*"

Silently I questioned, "wear a tie? What does that have to do with my salvation?" I hated ties, and I only wore them to church. Then, I asked him, "*Do you mean I should wear a tie every day?*" He answered, "Yes," with pastoral guidance and conviction. I didn't sign up for this when I got saved, I thought to myself, and I was unhappy with the pastor's suggestion.

I believed if I wore a tie regularly, it would change my self-image. People would see me differently in an unfamiliar way. I had become comfortable with myself, and I liked my self-image. Nonetheless, I heeded my spiritual leader's instruction.

I didn't realize the pastor had my spiritual growth in mind, and that he was encouraging me to become Christ-like. Yes, I had become a new creation in Christ and things were different. I needed to reflect the changes, but I knew very little about transformation. My obedience to the pastor's recommendation paid off, and something like a miracle happened.

Shortly after I began wearing a tie every day, a new employment opportunity became available at my job. I applied for the position, and within two or three months, I got the job. That convinced me my professional appearance made a difference! Several years later, I retired in a professional capacity with the same employer. God's grace brought me that far!

Soon in the church, the senior pastor asked me to be an assistant Sunday School teacher, and I was again dumbfounded. I didn't know how to teach the Bible, and I wondered what I was supposed to do? I relied on the Holy Spirit, and I fell in love with learning, The Bible, and teaching others. I regularly taught in Sunday School, and the Junior Church. Later I was appointed to be a theology instructor in our church's institute. God's grace, mercy, and love allowed me to impact the church and the world.

"All this is from God, who through Christ reconciled us to himself and gave us the ministry of reconciliation"
(2 Corinthians 5:17).

37

The Valley of Death

I desired to return to college and complete my undergraduate degree after I converted to Christ. I promised God that what I learned in college, I'd use it to help the church, community, and bring him glory. I was excited to resume my education, and I attended school part-time and worked full-time. There were many tests and trials during that period in my life.

Contrary to my expectations, one of the most unnerving classes was named 'The African-American Family.' The course involved a myriad of topics and lectures about the African American diaspora, the enslavement of Africans in the United States and the British colonies. The course was exasperating!

My adjunct professor, a former member of the Black Panther political organization, was a short, slender, and light-skinned somber-looking black woman. She thoroughly knew the course's content, and it seemed like black militancy exuded from her DNA. Mrs. Taylor, the professor, unflinchingly revealed the painful truths of the not so distant African American experience marred by slavery, oppression, and racism. I was devastated by the facts of the diaspora and the systemic devolution of the black family, especially its males. The realities affected me emotionally, and I was depressed and demoralized. I became suicidal. On top of that, I experienced a vitiating experience in my church.

At some point, my biological family and I attended the same church where my mother served as a missionary and Sunday School teacher. My mother assisted other local ministries as well, but one day she was given an ultimatum per church policy. She was asked to either terminate her involvement with the other ministries or face excommunication from our congregation. My mother loved to help people, so reluctantly, she decided to continue her work outside our local congregation. The situation was devastating to me, and it was difficult to imagine worshipping in church without her.

My mother was involved in my life after she placed me for adoption, and she maintained a surrogate role while I grew up. She was always available to my adoptive parents and me when we needed her for guidance. She prayed for me to get saved after she became born again, and when I got saved, she and I grew closer and bonded significantly. God's grace was healing our relationship, and it was challenging to be separated from her again. My world collapsed after she decided to leave our congregation, and I felt like I plunged into the valley of death!

I was overcome by the reality of racism, social devaluation, and family separation. I despaired of life, and the dark forces of suicide gripped me. It seemed I wouldn't survive, but thanks be to God, I came this far by his grace!

"Even though I walk through the valley of the shadow of death, I will fear no evil, for you are with me"
(Psalm 23:4).

38

W

Can a Christian
Have a Demon?

*"For we do not wrestle against flesh and blood, but against the
rulers, against authorities, against the cosmic powers over this
present darkness, against the spiritual forces in heavenly places"*
(Ephesians 6:12).

I continued the college course, and the historical realities were
more unnerving with each class. My consciousness was paralyzed
by disparagement and fear, and my mother's expulsion from our
ministry added to the anxiety. As the powers of darkness and
suicide haunted me I was confused. I was a Christian.

My suicidal ideations were not the result of drugs and alcohol
or other sins. I was a new creation in Jesus Christ, buried with
him in his death and raised to newness of life in his resurrection
(Romans 6:4). I wondered what was wrong. The problem was that
sin has affected us all, and I was in a spiritual battle.

Sin has affected every aspect of our lives, and it broke God's "shalom" or peace. It has marred the creation, and things are not the way God created them to be. Personally, I experienced the insidious effects of the spiritual enemy named Satan (the devil) in whom sin originated (Isaiah 14:12-17). Not only did Satan acquiesce to become like God, but he also embarked on a mission to kill, steal, and destroy God's creation and created ones.

I discovered that Satan and his demons could not "possess" a born-again believer, but the devil's forces and demonic spirits can "oppress" (harass, intimidate, persecute and torment) a Christian to the point that one despairs of life. I was on that tipping point, but I was not ready to give up or die! The Lord had plans for my life, and I realized he had been with me in all my pitfalls.

I needed to trust that he wouldn't abandon and leave me now in the valley. With an elusive strand of hope, I had to believe God's grace would rescue me from the abyss of death. I kept my faith in Jesus Christ, and I came this far by grace.

"My grace is sufficient for you, for my power
is made perfect in weakness"
(2 Corinthians 12:9).

39

Faith as a Mustard Seed

"And she begged him to cast the demon out of her daughter...And she went home and found the child lying in bed and the demon gone"
(Mark 7:26-30).

I still had a grain of faith, although I was tormented over America's apartheid, and the antagonism my religious institution inflicted on my family. I held on to Jesus, but it was a time of spiritual warfare like I had not experienced. It was out of this world! Christ himself had dealings with the spiritual underworld.

Jesus Christ, the Creator of all things, understood the realities of the spiritual world better than we comprehend. Jesus not only had supernatural ability to rebuke the boisterous wind and sea (Mark 4:39), but he also expelled demons out of people on several occasions (Matthew 4:24, 15:25-28; Luke 8:1-2 and 26-33). Jesus' *"deliverance ministry"* validated that he was the Messiah (Matthew 12:22-28).

Jesus knew that sin, Satan, and demons seek to disrupt, disorder, and destroy peoples' lives, and the administration of deliverance (driving out evil spirits) was a significant part of Christ's earthly ministry. His involvement in deliverance helped convey that all believers are inducted into spiritual warfare. "Put on the whole armor of God, that you may be able to stand against the schemes of the devil. For we do not wrestle against flesh and blood, but against the rulers, against the authorities, against the cosmic powers over this present darkness, against the spiritual forces of evil in the heavenly places" (Ephesians 6:11-12), the Apostle Paul wrote.

I had committed those verses to memory, but I wondered if I'd be freed from the torment I had experienced for the past few months. I grew angry, seemingly no one in church realized I was struggling to stay alive as I sat in the pews and sang in the choir. Then, a miracle happened just when I thought I might give up.

It was towards the end of a Sunday evening church service when my miracle occurred. I knew the lady who came to minister that night. She was a minister who had a testimony of overcoming several years of cocaine addiction, and she became an evangelist after she was born again. She was a mighty servant of God, and the Holy Spirit gave her a beautiful, gracious gift to reach lost and hopeless people. She served and directed our church's food pantry and homeless ministry. It was towards the conclusion of her service that I received my miracle.

The evangelist closed her Bible after concluding the gospel message, and she walked away from the place where she had ministered. She walked to the front of the church, and then she asked the congregation if anyone wanted to be prayed for. I was so desperate until I don't remember getting up and going for a prayer. With my grain of faith, I found myself in front of the church.

Immediately, I gained the evangelist's attention, and she walked over and stood directly in front of me. Then, she placed her hand on my forehead and anointed my head with oil before she prayed. As she leaned forward to pray, she quietly said these words in my ears, *"Come out in the name of Jesus!"* As soon as I heard the words (*"come out in the name of Jesus)*, something happened to me. It felt like a belt, a harness, or tether had been loosed from an area below my waist. I experienced something physically and supernaturally. Then, I was convinced that invisible Satanic forces had constrained me and provoked me to depression and suicide. After the evangelist prayed, I knew I was free! The power of the Holy Spirit and the name of Jesus made me free.

The week following, another evangelist stationed in our local church assembly, prayed for me. I don't think she said anything, but simply she placed her hand on my head and prayed. I felt confident that my healing and deliverance were secure. The devil has tried to hinder and thwart God's plans and purposes in many ways.

The spiritual warfare I encountered, it substantiated for me that a Christian can be afflicted by demonic influences and entities. But Satan's power is limited and subject to God's sovereignty. The Holy Spirit is more powerful, and through the ages, God's grace (unmerited favor) has helped people overcome and live productively and meaningfully as God prescribed. Jesus has made his followers more than conquerors. His grace is enough!

"..I have said these things to you, that in me you may have peace. In this world you will have tribulation. But take heart; I have overcome the world"
(John 16:33).

40

🔥

An Overcomer's Prayer

If you believe you are valueless, and your life is not worth living, then pray the following Overcomer's Prayer:

Father God, you are good, great, and kind. I believe you are the Creator of all things, including me. You know every hair on my head, and you made me in your image and likeness. Everything you make is good, so I am valuable to you and others. You are love, and you created me to honor and represent you in the world! Lord, I believe your plans and purposes are incredible, and that you created me to be a part of your comprehensive project in the world. I am not a mistake, and I am fearfully and wonderfully made. Help me to learn and not neglect or forget your many promises in the Bible. I want to live and not die! Help me to make being a part of your Kingdom and obtaining your righteousness my priority. Thank you for sending Jesus to die for my sins and to save me! I give you the glory, honor, and praise. I ask all these things in Jesus, our Savior's Name.
Amen.

41

In the Kingdom!

"Lift up your heads, O gates..that the King of glory may come in. Who is this King of glory? The Lord of hosts, he is the King of glory"
(Psalm 24:9–10).

Finally, I realized God had called me to be a minister of Jesus Christ, just as Deacon Jones prophesied when I was young. I avoided God's calling for many years, but eventually, I resigned to do his will. First, I was ordained a Bible teacher, and then a minister (licensed to preach), and God blessed me with many desires of my heart. I was also given the opportunity to glorify him in the local community.

After I earned my college degree, I was hired as a probation officer, and I worked with delinquent youths in the southside communities I grew up in. I found the career rewarding, and an awesome opportunity to give back. It became apparent, however, that the youths in the family court needed more than criminal justice measures to help them successfully navigate life.

I envisioned myself in a ministry with the kids, and I wanted to teach the Bible to them. A senior probation officer had said to me, "Make sure you give them (the youths) a big dose of religion," I laughed and said that I would! One of the youths attended a drug treatment facility in upstate New York. Little did I know, the facility was located less than twenty minutes from where I lived.

When I called the drug counselor to get a report on the kid's progress, I suddenly remembered a dream I had had six months earlier. I had dreamed I was escorted down a short hallway in a collegiate gothic-styled building, and it was a bright sunny afternoon. From the hallway corridor, I noticed several classrooms with flip-top desks. Then, I woke up from the dream!

I pondered the dream for a while and perceived the Lord was calling me to another phase of the teaching ministry. "Hey, do you all have Bible studies for the youths in your facility?" I eagerly asked the drug counselor. "No, but we did in the past. Are you interested in starting a Bible study here?" he replied. Emphatically, I said, "Yes, I am!"

The drug counselor provided me with the probation information, and then he transferred my call to the director of the facility. Nervously and excitedly, I told the director I wanted to share with the youths my testimony of how I came to be a Christian. The director gave his consent, and the following Monday, I told my testimony to more than sixty-five teens struggling with some of the same problems I grappled with when I was their age. I told them how I overcame through salvation and God's grace, and I started a Bible study in the facility. The facility building resembled the one I saw in my dream.

The following year I resigned from my associate pastoral

position in the local church, and I started a parachurch ministry with the teens from the drug treatment facility. Soon, we had Bible studies, Sunday School, and church services every week. My life was not the same, and I learned a lot about myself as I ministered to the youths. I realized that like them, I had been "a troubled kid," and it was indeed God's grace and plan that I minister to them. I had hope for the young people and the rest of the world because with God nothing was impossible!

The Lord opened other doors for me to explain his word, proclaim the truth, and encourage people to be changed by Jesus' redeeming work of grace. I wanted everyone to know that Jesus is the answer for the world today. He brought us this far by grace and for his purpose.

"For we are his workmanship created in Christ Jesus for good works, which God prepared beforehand, that we should walk in them (Ephesians 2:10).

42

A Thousand Words!

Hardly, I could believe I was in the pulpit in Calvary Baptist Church in Eastman, Virginia. I had not been to the church, but things seemed familiar as I stood in the pulpit in 2004. People told me that Calvary Baptist had been our family church for years, and it was where David Ellis, my biological father, attended Sunday School and was baptized. Now, more than sixty years later, both he and I were there for his eulogy. I looked around the church and hoped to find a clue to his past. David's life was a mystery to me.

When I met Aunt Margret, David's older sister, she told me that my father was the youngest of their siblings and that their father, Grandpa Cliff, abandoned the family when David was very young. Employed as a railroad conductor, purportedly Grandpa Cliff left his family in Eastman, Virginia, and he relocated to Washington, D.C. where he started a new family. Grandpa Cliff was not involved in David's life, and I discovered my father was the product of a dysfunctional household.

I glanced back and forth at David's reposed, almost

boyish-looking corpse dressed in a black pinned striped suit, and I took a last look at him before I settled down for the eulogy. My eyes shifted to his obituary program I held in my hand and David's picture on the front of the leaflet. The picture was probably fifty years old, but it grabbed my attention.

David, handsome in his early years, had impressive light brown eyes, but his eyes looked incredibly sad in the picture. As I stared at his photo, the words *lonely, abandoned, angry, unaffirmed, hopeless, and sad,* came to mind. David's picture spoke a thousand words to me that day.

For the first time, it seemed like I learned who my biological father was, and I realized he had suffered from abandonment and rejection as I did. No wonder he hadn't acknowledged or accepted me as his son. I wanted to hug him and tell him that I loved him, and I understood, but it was too late for that, David had passed away.

43

It's Not Over!

It felt surreal that Parris, my paternal half-sister, had invited me to Calvary Baptist Church to perform the eulogy for our father's funeral. I hadn't had much of a meaningful relationship with our father, but since I was ten years old, I knew who he was. I remembered the day my adoptive father, Lee Johnson, told me about David Ellis.

Daddy and I were riding in the elevator to our sixth-floor apartment, and bluntly, I asked him, *"Daddy, who is my real father?"* It was the umpteen time I asked, but that time Dad surprised me. He replied, *"You know the man who parks his car a couple of spaces from my parking spot?"* I said, *"Yes,"* and Dad just smiled and fell silent. I was shocked with disbelief. I had no idea my birth father was someone I knew, not to mention that he lived in our neighborhood!

My birth father and his family lived in one of the neighboring project buildings in our small southside community, and I couldn't imagine he didn't know who I was. I saw him almost every day.

He always spoke to my dad, and it seemed impossible to me that a person could have a child and not say "hi" to him. I felt I needed to get even, and I planned to do it by introducing myself. I would be the first one to say hello. Fifteen years later, I introduced myself to David Ellis.

One afternoon, I saw David talking to my uncle-in-law, Larry Winn. I had learned that Uncle Larry and David grew up together in Eastman, Virginia, where they went to school and were best friends. The day I saw the two of them talking to each other, I thought it was an opportunity to meet my father.

Dressed in skinny jeans, clog shoes, and with natural blond-streaked hair, I walked courageously up to Uncle Larry and said hello. He paused from his conversation with David, and he greeted me. I made some small talk with Uncle Larry about a repair he was doing for the Johnsons, and I asked him when I could pick up the table. When he and I finished talking, I anxiously said, "Thanks, Uncle Larry, I'll see you later." David Ellis didn't say anything to me, but I felt some relief. I wondered if I'd have another opportunity to confront him.

A few months later, I confronted David in a local nightclub. Carelessly inebriated, I introduced myself to him and started a conversation as if we had been friends, all our lives. He didn't know what to say, and it was embarrassing for both of us. But I was desperate to know him even if it meant making a fool of myself. That night was a sham, but by God's grace, I gained closure with David six months before he died.

44

🔥

Better Late Than Never!

More than ten years passed before I spoke to David after our night club rendezvous! Our lives had changed. I was born-again, involved in the ministry and my career. David had aged, and he lived alone. I had called him a couple of times in the past, but on Mother's Day 2004, the Holy Spirit instigated something remarkable.

For a few days, the Holy Spirit urged me to call David. I tried to dismiss the Spirit's compulsion, but the Holy Spirit was persistent. Finally, I obeyed.

I called David ("Pop") one evening as I was about to leave work. It had been years, but quickly and nervously, I dialed the telephone number I had. The phone rang three times on the other end, and a recording came on. *"Your call is being forwarded to (area code…telephone number…)"* I thought I dialed the wrong number, but before I hung up, a young woman answered the phone.

Surprised, I responded, *"God bless you. Um, may I speak to*

David" I asked? In a puzzled tone, the woman inquired, *"Who are you?"* *"Minister Donald Johnson,"* I said. Defensively, she asked me how I knew her grandfather, and I was stunned. I swallowed hard like I did when Dad told me David was my birth father, and I said to her, *"Um, Um, I'm his (David's) son."* It sounded like the young lady dropped the phone. She, my paternal niece did not know me, but she paused and then said excitedly, *"I'm going to call my mother."* I asked her not to do so, but she insisted. Minutes later, I was on the phone with her mother, Parris Ellis-Davis.

I knew Parris was my sister since I was ten years old. She was a couple years older, and often I saw her in the park in our community. I wondered if we'd ever meet. When she and I met, she told me she had not heard of me before my phone call. Parris and I grew close, and she informed me also that our father, David Ellis, was in a nursing home, a few blocks from where I worked. I was convinced the Holy Spirit was working in our family situation. I went to see our father as soon as I got off the phone with Parris.

Mother Susan, David's former wife, was in the hospital room when I arrived. I was surprised to see her because I thought she and David were divorced. I couldn't believe this was happening.

Every step I took inside the hospital room seemed like a milestone as I walked up to David's bedside. "Hi David," I said. He smiled at me and then looked up at Mother Susan. With a long overdue confession, he said to her, "They say he (me) is my son." I was shocked. It was the first time I heard him acknowledge the idea he was my father. I resembled my biological dad a lot, and when I became a teenager, my aunt Penny used to say to me, "You look just like David!" At age fifty, I still looked like him, and by my appearance, it was undeniable I was his son. I was closer to ending a chapter in my life than before.

Shortly after that, Parris relocated our father to live with her and her daughter in Washington. David phoned me a few times, and he always seemed apologetic. I felt sorry for him as he haphazardly tried to be a father to me during the last days of his life. David went into the hospital in Washington, and I went to visit him before he died.

There was a stillness in David's dimly lit hospital room in D.C. Pop looked palled and thin from a distance, but his crouched body was recognizable from the doorway. He managed to smile as I walked to his bedside, but soon his grin dissolved as he grimaced with pain from lung and liver cancers. I smiled back at him as I stood by his bed, and I asked him how he felt. I figured it would be the last time I'd see him alive, and I needed to talk to him about salvation. "Pop," I said, "Have you thought about being saved? Born again?" He replied honestly and said, "I'm thinking about it." He and I prayed after, which rather abruptly, he directed his attention to me.

He said a few things that surprised me. He started affirming me as a caring son and a child of God. I couldn't believe it because, for fifty years, I had needed that. But I praised God and gave God the glory. I thought, "it's better late than never." I left the hospital with peace and a sense of wholeness. David died a few days later, and during his eulogy in Calvary Baptist Church, I prayed that David Ellis, our father, was at rest.

"I will restore to you the years that the swarming locust has eaten..And my people shall never again be put to shame"
(Joel 2:25-26).

45

First, the test, then the Lesson!

*"Blessed is the man who remains steadfast under trial,
for when he has stood the test he will receive the crown
of life which God promised to those that love him"*
(James 1:12).

The first time I traveled to the Philippines for ministry work, I heard a proverb on a local radio program. The radio host said, *"Wisdom is a hard teacher; the test comes first, and then the lesson."* I smiled as I thought how true the saying was.

Often, I did not understand why God allowed the tests and trials I encountered in my life, but I learned valuable lessons from the tests I endured. I thought about the tests I failed and had to repeat over and over, and I realized God wanted me to learn a lesson each time. Sometimes, I've considered life is one big test that we either pass or fail.

I regretted I allowed sin to depredate my life for so long and that it caused my heart to be deceived and callous. My life changed tragically, and I failed miserably because of sin and selfishness. But thanks be to God, I have come this far by grace, and I learned many valuable lessons.

One of the greatest lessons I've learned is that God's word is the truth, and his ways and plans are best. By accepting Jesus Christ and God's holiness and standards of living, it enabled me to discard the negative patterns and ideologies to which I had succumbed. Becoming a Christian has involved me changing (transformation) and seeking Christ's mind and Kingdom daily. For as long as we live, we are learning and changing!

The apostle Paul learned many things from his religious upbringing and Jewish heritage. He was an instructor protecting the strict religious observances of the Mosaic laws, and in his enforcements, he rejected Christ and persecuted people who followed Jesus. But the Holy Spirit intervened in Paul's life, and he became a teacher of the truth and a disciple of Christ.

God showed Paul that he was trying to serve the Lord the wrong way. "And falling to the ground, he heard a voice saying to him, 'Saul, Saul, why are you persecuting me? And he said, 'Who are you, Lord? And he said, 'I am Jesus, whom you are persecuting" (Acts 9:4-5). Resulting from Paul's divine encounter with the risen Christ, he surrendered his life to Jesus, and he recognized he had some unlearning to do. Often, God's plans have been different than those we've envisioned and idealized for our life's goals.

Later, in his letter to the Philippians, Paul confessed, "But whatever gain I had, I counted as loss for the sake of Christ. Indeed, I count everything as loss because of the surpassing worth of knowing Christ Jesus my Lord" (Philippians 3:7-8). Many times, we are tempted to rely on our resources and deviate from God's plans, but if we allow him to tutor us and refine us through testing, we will learn eternal lessons.

"For as the heavens are higher than the earth, so are my ways higher than your ways and my thoughts than your thoughts"
(Isaiah 55:9).

46

In Sum!

"The end of the matter; all has been heard. Fear God and keep his commandments for this is the whole duty of man"
(Ecclesiastes 12:13).

I was born into a difficult situation in an era of immense social and cultural changes. Rapidly, the world changed while I grappled with emotional problems and identity conflicts. As an adopted child, I struggled to understand my place in the world, family, and community. Like a misfit, I felt emotionally displaced and experienced unexplainable grief, anger, and sadness. I was deceived by youthful invincibility, sexual promiscuity, alcohol and drugs, and other vices which I thought alleviated my pain. But my situation didn't get better, and I went from bad to worse.

I worried about being accepted and rejected, and I looked for affirmation and love in people, places, groups, and things. I made excuses for my lack of personal responsibility, and I looked to escape through the counterculture. After I was diagnosed with a Substance Abuse-Induced Psychotic Disorder[28] and the potential for borderline schizophrenia, I admitted I had serious problems for which I needed real help.

I was confronted with the reality in an abyss of homelessness, psychiatric institutionalizations, and hopelessness. I had to decide to either stay in the pit or head for "the palace-" God's Kingdom. It was not an easy choice to make.

I was thirty-five years old, and I had spent so many years living a riotous and unproductive life. I thought about my ruined reputation, arrest history, and the sordid past that no one else and I would forget. But I began to trust God, and I learned how to hope again! I started "to let go and let God," and finally, I accepted the fact I needed to be born-again.

Far from Father God and my true self, I remembered the words in Psalm 23, and I rehearsed the verses while I sat alone in the psych ward. Glory to God, it was a defining moment for me, I was done! The time had come, and with a grain of faith, I asked the Lord to save and reclaim me. I surrendered to Christ, and I told him I'd serve him the rest of my life. I hummed the words to one of the church songs I heard when I was growing up, *"Father, I stretch my hands to thee; no other help; no other help I know."* God helped me!

Released from the psychiatric hospital a few days later and before the New Year, I was at the church altar when the new year came in. I celebrated my emancipation from spiritual slavery and from Satan as my master. I had made Jesus my Lord, and Christ's perfect and righteous rule would govern me the rest of my days. I gave him glory and thanked him for bringing me this far by grace!

*"The law of the LORD is perfect, reviving the soul; the testimony
of the LORD is sure making wise the simple..Let the words
of my mouth and the meditation of my heart be acceptable
in your sight, O LORD, my rock and my redeemer"*
(Psalm 19:7, 14).

47

The End

"Through many dangers, toils and snares, we have already come. Twas grace that brought us safe thus far. And grace will lead us home..Amazing grace, how sweet the sound that saved a wretched like me. I once was lost but now am found, was blind, but now I see"
(John Newton, 1772).

It has been a joy to share my story. Sometimes it was painful, even appalling, to recollect how God saved me. I've wondered how I survived, but I know it was God's grace that brought me to where I am today. The day I turned from my ways of living (repented), and set my heart on God and Jesus, my life and everything around me changed!

I realized that God sent Christ into the world to save people from their sins. We can be forgiven, made righteous, and have eternal life. Providentially protected and saved by God's grace, he turned my gloom into his glory. Thank you, Jesus, for making my life a living testimony of your unmerited favor and inexhaustible grace! Glory to God.

I pray by reading my true story, you will understand and believe that the Lord Jesus Christ can save anyone and help him or her overcome their problems. There is no struggle that God cannot remediate or a problem he cannot fix. You can be an overcomer, more than a conqueror, as you passionately pursue Christ with all your heart, soul, mind, and strength.

If you have not received Jesus Christ as your Savior, and you want to be saved, I invite you to pray the following prayer:

Father God, you are good! Righteous and holy, you love the world. You proved it by sending Jesus, the Lamb of God who takes away the sin of the world. I believe Jesus is your Son; that he died for my sins, and your power raised him from the dead. I am sorry for my sins, and I ask you to forgive me. Jesus save me, and I will be saved. Heal me, and I will be healed. Fill me with your Holy Spirit and give me a brand-new life; And I will give you the honor, the glory, and the praise.

In Jesus' Name! Amen.

We've all come this far by grace, and still, the best is yet to happen.

"Then I saw a new heaven and a new earth..And I heard a loud voice from the throne saying, Behold the dwelling place of God is with man. He will dwell with them, and they will be his people, and God himself will be with them as their God. He will wipe away every tear from their eyes, and death shall be no more"
(Revelation 21:1-4).
Amen!

END NOTES

1   Millard J. Erickson, *Christian Theology* (Grand Rapids, Michigan: Baker Book House Company, 1985), 294-95.

2   Ibid, 294.

3   Judith Schachter, "Adoption," in *The Child an Encyclopedic Companion*, ed. Richard A. Shweder (Chicago: University of Chicago Press, 2009), 23-25.

4   Ibid, 25.

5   ESV Study Bible, *Introduction to Esther* (Wheaton, Illinois: Crossway, 2008), 850-52.

6   Anne C. Dailey, "Legal and Public Policy Perspectives" in *The Child : An Encyclopedic Companion* (Chicago: University of Chicago Press, 2009), 149.

7   Adoptions with Love Incorporated, a registered 501(c)(3) organization, www.adoptionwithlove.org/adoption/agency, info@awlonline.org.

8   Ibid.

9   Ibid.

10   James Garbarino, *Lost Boys* (New York: The Free Press, 1999), 43-45.

11   *Brown vs Board of Education*,2009 URL-http://www.history.com/topics/black-history/brown-v-board-of-education-of-topeka, Access Date: December 23, 2018, Publisher: A+E Networks https://www.history.com/topics

12   *Children receive first polio vaccine*,History.com 2010, URL:http://www.history.com/this-day-in-history/children-receive-first-polio-vaccine, Access Date August 23, 2018.

13   *Webster's New World College Dictionary*, 4th Edition (Cleveland, Ohio: Wiley Publishing, Inc.), 2007.

14   Samuel Smith, "Sexuality a 'Counter-Gospel' in today's culture, Russell Moore argues in New Book," *The Christian Post*, September 18, 2018, accessed October 30, 2019, www.christianpost.com/books/sexuality-sounter-gospel-culture-russell-morre-book-storm-tossed-family.html.

15   Douglas Martin, "David Cohen is Dead at age 80," June 2, 2002, https://www.nytimes.com/2002/06/02/nyregion/david-cohen-is-dead-at-80-led-chain-of-bargain-stores.html, accessed July 1, 2019.

16   "*Mark Twain (Samuel Clemens)*, The Prince and The Pauper," The Project Gutenberg EBook,2006 https://www.gutenberg.org/files/1837/1837-h/1837-h.htm, accessed March 12, 2019.

17   *Wikipedia*. "The civil rights movement." https://en.wikipedia.org/wiki/Civil_rights_movement, accessed January 30, 2019.

18   (macro history and world timeline. http://www.fsmitha.com/time/1964.htm).

19   *Wikipedia*. "Counter-culture of the 1960s." https://en.wikipedia.org/wiki/Counterculture_o_the_1960s, accessed May 15, 2019.

20   Ibid.

21   A quote by Jen Pollock Michel, https://www.jenpollockmichel.com

22   "Substance use-amphetamines." https://medlineplus.gov/ency/patientinstructions/000792.htm

23   *Webster's New World College Dictionary, 4th Ed.*

24   https://www.britannica.com/topic/Watch-Night, recently revised and updated by Lorraine Murray, Associate Editor.

25   Ibid.

26   Ibid.

27   John Piper, *"What Is Discipleship and How Is It Done?"* https://www.desiringgod.org/interviews/what-is-discipleship-and-how-is-it-done. Accessed May 21, 2019.

28   American Psychiatric Association: *Diagnostic and Statistical Manual of Mental Disorders*, 4th ed, Text Revision. (Washington, DC: American Psychiatric Association, 2000), 338.

Printed in the United States
By Bookmasters